FOOTSTEPS AND WITNESSES

FOOTSTEPS AND WITNESSES

LESBIAN AND GAY LIFESTORIES FROM SCOTLAND

EDITED BY
BOB CANT

POLYGON
EDINBURGH

© Polygon 1993

First published by Polygon
22 George Square
Edinburgh

Set in Weiss
by ROM-Data Corporation Ltd, Falmouth, Cornwall
Printed and bound in Great Britain by
Short Run Press Ltd, Exeter

A CIP record for this book is available from the British Library

ISBN 0 7486 6170 0

The Publisher acknowledges subsidy from the
Scottish Arts Council towards the publication of this volume.

CONTENTS

ACKNOWLEDGMENTS

Thanks are due to all the people who helped to make this book a reality

– to the Scottish Arts Council for providing financial assistance towards travel and research;

– to Marion Sinclair and Kathryn MacLean at Polygon for their support and commitment;

– to all those who helped me make contact with interviewees and offered me help and encouragement when I needed it – Mark Allan, John Binnie, Maggie Christie, Bruce Cochran, Susan Elsley, Peter Harrower, Susan Hemmings, Eric Kay, Michael Keates, Iona McGregor, Linda McQueen, Bob Orr, David Southey, Alistair Stevenson, John Warburton, Christopher Whyte, Andrew Wilson, Ewan Wilson, Graeme Woolaston;

– to Anne Boyle for typing the transcripts efficiently and with gusto;

– to John Binnie, Seamus Prior and Gwen Williams who each conducted two interviews;

– to all the interviewees who agreed to share their stories with the world.

I am the person responsible for the finished product, flaws and all, but without all their support and love, there would have been no book.

Footsteps and witnesses: In this Glasgow balcony who pours
such joy like mountain water? It brims, it spills over and over
down to the parched earth and the relentless wheels.
How often will I think of you, until
our dying steps forget this light, forget
that we ever knew the happy glen,
or that I ever said, We must jump into the sun,
and we jumped into the sun.

Extract: *From A City Balcony* by Edwin Morgan

INTRODUCTION

Lesbians and gay men are, for the most part, invisible in Scotland. The few public references that are made to us – by teachers, by preachers, by politicians, by pundits – imply that we are Other, that we are 'these people', that we do not belong. This book is part of a collective process which began in the late 1960s to end that invisibility. It is part of a process that has endeavoured to make it clear that lesbians and gay men are an integral part of Scottish society. This book, by bringing together a collection of diverse lifestories, is a kind of coming out.

Silence in the public arena has been a major mode of control of homosexual people both in Scotland and in the UK as a whole. A major turning-point in the history of silencing was the publication of the Wolfenden Report in 1957. The report recommended the de-criminalization of sexual activity between consenting adult males. The publication of the report unleashed a media discussion about homosexual lifestyles unknown since the Oscar Wilde trials in 1895. As a twelve year-old boy living in rural Angus, I read about the Wolfenden Report in the *Dundee Courier* and it was there that I first saw the word, homosexuality, in print for the first time. It helped me to give a name to the confused sexual feelings I was beginning to experience. Isolated though I was, I was just one of many, both male and female, who benefitted from this debate about homosexuality.

The Scottish press of the time was overwhelmingly opposed to Wolfenden's recommendations. They agreed with the minority position taken by James Adair, a Scottish member of the Royal Commission which had produced the report. Adair was a Church of Scotland elder and a former Procurator Fiscal of Glasgow. He accused many of the advisers to the Commission of displaying a 'marked degree of sentimentalism'. He saw de-criminalization as leading to an openness in homosexual lifestyles and warned:

> 'the presence of adult male lovers living openly
> and notoriously under the approval of the law is
> bound to have a regrettable and pernicious effect
> on the young people of the community.'

The support in the press and in other Scottish institutions for this view helped to ensure that the legislation to de-criminalize male homosexual activity in Scotland did not happen until 1980.

Adair's role in this can be interpreted in a number of ways. Firstly, he can be seen as an authentic voice of the Calvinist tradition. Dating back to the sixteenth century, Calvinism had been the mainstay of the struggle to keep Scottish society both democratic and homogenous. With the departure of the Parliament in 1707 and the end of the opportunity to make laws in Scotland, the Kirk had had a pivotal role at the centre of civil society. The Calvinist values and regulations it perpetrated had prevented Scotland from becoming a colonial outpost composed of disaffected and alienated individuals. Adair, according to this view, was simply defending Scotland from yet another alien and unchristian incursion.

While I accept some of the argument about the role of the Kirk in civil society, I see Adair in a less favourable light. The Kirk's central position had been maintained to some extent because of its success in suppressing or assimilating other Christian tendencies, whether Roman Catholic, Episcopalian or Free Presbyterian. Adair represented that authoritarian tradition and his opposition to the de-criminalization of male homosexual activity was based on a desire to maintain the status quo and to preserve a culture of deference and fear.

Prior to Wolfenden, the only public references to homosexuality in Scotland had been through humour or verbal abuse. Homosexual activity was known to occur in particular circumstances and places, such as in bothys or boys' schools, and while it was never condoned, neither was it systematically persecuted. The reporting of cases of 'gross indecency' between men was uncommon in the local press and there were no great show-trials in the 1950s and 1960s such as there were in England. For those who wanted to form a homosexual relationship based on more than casual sexual activity, exile was the most attractive option. For those who chose to remain in Scotland, the weapon of silence ensured that they did so in conditions of isolation.

The tyranny of silence in Scotland was broken in 1969 with the establishment of the Scottish Minorities Group (SMG). Later known as the Scottish Homosexual Rights Group and now as *Outright*, this group, led by gay men, became the key pressure group for homosexual law reform. A programme of lobbying and tactical alliances by SMG succeeded in having homosexual activity by consenting male adults de-criminalized in 1980. Obliged as it was to lobby Westminster-based MPs, SMG never became a mass political movement within Scotland itself. SMG, in fact, had a dual identity. It was both a small band of high-profile urban activists and a much larger, looser network of women and men in cities and towns across the country. SMG was the stimulus which enabled many lesbians and gay men to come out of their isolation and to meet one another.

The period following 1969 was remarkable in many other ways too. Scotland, along with the rest of Western Europe, had enjoyed an improved standard of living since the end of the Second World War. Free health services, decent housing, full (male) employment and increased consumer spending were all generating different expectations from those that were commonplace before the war. People, especially young people, wanted more choice in the way they lived their lives and many were able to benefit from the expansion of further and higher education. The availability of the contraceptive Pill from the 1960s onwards meant that heterosexual men and, more particularly, women, had the opportunity to be sexually active in a way that had been previously denied them. Scotland in this sense participated in an international social and sexual revolution.

The late 1960s was also the beginning of the period which has seen the destruction of much of Scotland's heavy industrial base, the mechanization of agriculture and the diminution of the fishing industry. Unemployment and the casualization of employment have led to the pauperization or dispersal of many of the communities which provided the workforce for these industries. Such communities lost their economic focus and the familial and communal ties which had held them together were weakened, sometimes irrevocably. Relations between women and men have been transformed as a result. Men can no longer rely on security of employment sufficient to enable them to take on the breadwinner's role in the traditional way. Women can no longer rely on the networks of support and protection from male violence they might have had in more traditional communities.

Greater expectations, combined with structural economic change have both required and enabled individuals to make major life choices and in this respect they differ from their parents' generation. Homosexual people have, within this context, increasingly refused to suppress their sexuality. Lesbians and gay men are, in ever greater numbers, opting for honesty and for living their lives on their own terms. The industrialized world has seen the emergence of assertive and confident lesbian and gay communities; Scotland has been no stranger to this international process.

The last twenty-five years have also seen an extensive debate on the political future of Scotland. Since the election of Winnie Ewing as Scottish Nationalist MP for Hamilton in a 1967 by-election, the discontent about the lack of national political representation within Scotland has never been off the political agenda. All the political parties now locate themselves within a Scottish context as well as a UK context. Historians, sociologists and other commentators endlessly analyze the condition of Scottish society.

Support for some form of Scottish self-determination is neither conservative nor atavistic but the progressive elements within the movements for self-determination have largely failed to convey any understanding of the fact that Scotland is a pluralist society. The presence of substantial Asian and Chinese communities as well as other black and minority ethnic groups has failed to generate any meaningful anti-racist strand into the politics of self-determination. The most that black people and lesbians and gay men have been able to expect up to now is some tokenistic reference to the need to oppose discrimination. There has certainly been no enthusiasm from these self-determination debates about the politics of oppression. But when we compare Scotland today with Scotland in the days of James Adair, it is a million light years away.

There are, of course, people who still hold the same views Adair held but they cannot now command the unchallenged authority that he did. Scotland is now a pluralist society and any movement for self-determination, either within the UK or within the EC will have to take account of that pluralism.

The tradition of silence in the public arena means that students of homosexuality in Scotland are obliged to turn to popular culture and an oral history approach in ways that they have not been obliged to do in countries, such as England, which make their own laws. The evidence from popular culture may be fragmented and anecdotal but it does provide insight into the rich diversity of homosexual experience throughout the country. Plays performed, films seen, books and magazines read – all enable us to understand something about the pre-occupations and aspirations of the lesbian and gay communities.

As early as 1948, Glasgow Unity Theatre produced *The Lambs of God*, a play by Benedict Scott, about conflicts of desire in a poverty-stricken Scottish town. One of the two central characters is a man who openly defines himself as homosexual. The disastrous reception this finely-written play received tells us more about the régime of silence than it does about the play or its production. A speech by Dick, the homosexual character, conveys the sense of isolation so widely experienced by homosexual people at the time:

> 'Human companionship comes to me at street
> corners – or lounging across the bar at the *White*
> *Horse*. Once it moves on – I drift out of sight. And
> the bloody blindin' loneliness of it!'

Forty-five years later, Clyde Unity Theatre carries on the tradition of Glasgow Unity by writing plays about the lives of people in impoverished working class communities. Their gay characters are confronted by real, sometimes life or death, dilemmas but shame is not part of their vocabulary. Clyde Unity is only one of a number of sources of evidence illuminating the lives of the lesbian and gay communities today. West and Wilde bookshop in Edinburgh is another key place to find out what lesbians and gay men have on their minds. Students of popular culture could do worse than study the range of books and magazines sold there or by mail-order.

Beyond the world of theatre and publishing, there is a veritable goldmine of personal experience for the oral historian to explore. Every community had, and still has, individuals and couples whom everyone knew to be 'that way'. My earliest memory of a person who was alleged to be 'that way' was the woman with short hair and jacket and trousers who drove a van selling fish around the rural community where I lived. For a woman to be self-employed and to dress in such a fashion in the 1950s was to make a statement about something and the fish girl, as she was called, was widely believed to be making a statement about her sexuality. She was respected for the service that she provided and liked for her friendly manner far more than she was distrusted or shunned.

There is no fish girl in this book but there are people from a wide range of backgrounds. There are nurses, poets, youth-workers and teachers. There is a bowling alley manager, a farmer and a taxi driver. There are, not surprisingly for these recession-ravaged times, four unemployed people. There are both Catholics and Protestants; people born into the working classes and people born into the middle classes; black people and white people; incomers as well as native-born Scots. The oldest contributor was born in 1920 and the youngest in 1969. There is no part of Scotland that is untouched by the homosexual experience; contributors come from as far apart as Lewis and Dumfries, from Buckie and Fife as well as Scotland's major cities.

In general, women are excluded from much of the public arena in Scotland. Lesbians have also been excluded and silenced, not only on account of their sexuality, but also because of their gender. A strong revolutionary feminist network could be found in the East of Scotland in the late 1970s and early 1980s which identified patriarchal power as the central oppression in society. Many women from such a background would not want to be associated with a project, such as this book, which includes men. The law has never, formally at least, focused on lesbianism though it is often used as a justification to deprive women of custody of their children; there has, consequently, been a low level of involvement by lesbians in law reform campaigns. The continuing disparity between the earning power of women and men makes it more difficult for lesbians to participate fully in the commercially-run scene or generate their own scene. All these factors combine to give the oral history approach a particular significance in relation to recording and understanding the development of the lesbian communities. Informal networks are at the heart of the lesbian experience.

Most of the lesbians and many of the gay men have moved considerable distances from their communities of origin. Some moved away from Scotland altogether while they came to terms with their sexuality and resolved how they wished to express it. It is not unique to Scotland for people to leave their own communities to come to terms with their homosexuality but the lack of any metropolitan culture has been a major barrier to the growth of the lesbian and gay communities. That they have flourished as much as they have done in these circumstances in such a small country is a remarkable achievement.

Like many of the contributors, one of the reasons why I left Scotland was to enable me to establish some kind of gay lifestyle. During my twenty years in London, I began to feel distant from Scotland, my accent changed, and I often believed that I would never return. When I began the process of reconciliation in the late

1980s I was initially of the opinion that this would be limited to the level of the emotions. By 1990, however, I had found employment for myself in Scotland and decided to come home in a geographical as well as an emotional sense. For me this book was one stage in reconciling myself with a country from which I had become estranged.

The title, *Footsteps and Witnesses*, taken from the poem, *From a city balcony*, by Edwin Morgan illustrated some of the collective process of putting the book together. Aided by friends, and friends of friends, and people I never met, I searched for the footsteps or traces of lesbians and gay men in every part of the country. We found women and men who were prepared to act as witnesses not only to their own experience but also to the experiences of the wider communities of which they were part. Their acts of witness intensified my feeling that lesbians and gay men belong fully in Scotland.

The stories are remarkable, not because they are exceptional, but for their bravery, their sense of humour, their clarity of purpose, the strength of their love, their ingenuity; they are all remarkable for their integrity. It is these qualities that have helped our communities face up to the HIV epidemic which has killed so many gay men and renewed the power of prejudice and hostility against us. Even while recounting the pain that AIDS has inflicted on us, a sense of pride emerges from these stories. There is a sense of pride from all the contributors, whatever their ages and whatever their circumstances, of having created something worthwhile, something beautiful with their lives. All kinds of adversity, of which HIV and HIV-prejudice are but the most recent forms, have not succeeded in crushing that sense of pride.

There are many more lesbian and gay lifestories to be told. There are stories of struggles and campaigns and networks and love which are not included. This book does not purport to be *the* history book of Scotland's lesbian and gay communities in the twentieth century.

This book hopes to let the world know that these communities do have histories. This book is only a beginning.

Bob Cant
May 1993

EDWIN MORGAN

(b. 1920)

I was born in the West End of Glasgow, in Hyndland, in 1920. I was an only child and when I was two we moved south to Pollokshields. Later we moved to Rutherglen which is almost beyond Glasgow altogether. They were a well-doing family, church-going with a strong sense of responsibility. They were the kind of parents who watched out for your moral progress and so as an only child I grew up with a pretty strong sense of what was right and what was wrong. My mother would say – you may do something that we don't know about but there's an eye up there. I was very young and I remember looking up and imagining that eye was there. I grew up with that sense of conscience pretty strongly implanted.

My father worked with a firm of iron and steel merchants and he had, I suppose, a Calvinist businessman's idea. He took charge of the accounts and he was extremely hard-working, extremely honest, extremely conscientious and, perhaps going along with that, nervous. My mother was the same. She had that conscientiousness. I've got this nervousness still and I'm very easily made to feel that something is right or wrong.

There were other families with boys and girls of the same age round about and so I played with them in the usual way. We were in Albert Drive and I was even a member of an awful local football team called the Albertonians. I was never any good at football but you were expected to take part in group activities of that kind. I knew in myself that really wasn't my thing and maybe especially if you are an only child you tend to be by yourself and make up your own games. I collected stamps and then quite early on I began collecting words. I had a great list of words I would go through. My father would bring home gardening catalogues and I would make a list of the names of these strange, interesting plants. I don't know what I was going to do with these things but it must have been some kind of early pointer to the fact that I was going to use words myself. That was a solitary thing. I enjoyed doing that and then I kept scrap books when I was about eleven. I pasted things from newspapers and magazines into jotters and I did that for years. That is probably the kind of thing an only child would do rather than someone who grew up with brothers and sisters. My parents were very sensible and they didn't spoil me but you are, inevitably, I think, the centre of their interest. It probably takes you longer to rub along with other people than you would do if you had brothers and sisters but at the same time it has its own rewards in that you develop your own individuality.

I went to the local school in Rutherglen and I was there until I was fourteen when my parents thought I should sit a scholarship for Glasgow High School. The last three years of my schooling from fourteen to seventeen I was at Glasgow High School. The first school was a mixed school and the High School was a boys' school. I didn't like school but I did well. The subjects I enjoyed most were English and Art. I was very interested in abstract design. I used to do lots of paintings of designs that were simply patterns of different colours. There was a chance of getting an apprenticeship as a carpet designer at Templeton's carpet factory in Glasgow Green when I was about fifteen. Then when I took my Higher Art I almost decided to go to the School of Art in Glasgow. I was perhaps persuaded by some people that this wasn't a good idea and I went to university and took English. Even back to eleven or twelve, I wrote quite a lot and I think it was the right decision to carry on with the writing rather than the painting.

I knew in myself that probably the thing I enjoyed most was writing not just poems but essays. It was the life of the imagination that attracted me in writing and I tended to enjoy writers who were writing adventure stories set in far places, exotic adventure stories like Rider Haggard or science fiction stories like Jules Verne or somebody like Jack London. Things I wrote were often adventurous or set in exotic places. One of my early poems at school was called 'The Opium Smoker'. It probably comes from various things I'd read about the Far East and I enjoyed the imaginative appeal trying to imagine what this man's life would be like. The feeling I had was that whatever you write, it isn't enough just to describe what you see around you, there's got to be something coming from the imagination. It was mostly Romantic poetry we got at school – Keats and Tennyson and Shelley. That was the first poetry I liked and it wasn't realistic. It wasn't the kind of poetry I should have been reading as a person living in Glasgow in the Thirties. We started off with nineteenth-century literature and hardly came forward at all. It didn't encourage you to become any kind of realist in your writing. It took me a while to understand that you could write about any-thing – ugly things, dirty things, painful things. It can all be written about but no one told me that at school.

I was more aware of sex at the High School than I had been at Rutherglen Academy. Perhaps because it was a boys' school there was more of it going on. More relationships of various kinds – some platonic, some not platonic. More experimentation. I was very keen on a boy who was my opposite in some ways. He was sports captain of the school and we got on very well together. I used to help him with some of his problems in classwork and I had this great admiration for his physique and we often sat together. I suppose I maybe hoped that something would come of it but nothing ever did. I became sort of sexually active when we had a school trip to Germany in 1937. We were all told to wear the kilt and that obviously led to a good deal of sexual play which we all found very enjoyable and a lot of that went on in a way which was not all that furtive. The teachers seemed to regard it as something that was a part of your teens, that you would just grow out of. There was no great hassle about it. No scandals. It was something that was pleasurable and easy-going and it wasn't something that singled me out as a monster. It wasn't taken all that seriously and so I wasn't worried about it.

There were pressures when I was at the High School to meet girls. I remember being persuaded to join the local tennis club to meet girls. Of course, I did meet girls but it never led to anything. I had a very close friendship with a girl when I was at university and when I brought her home to meet my parents they presumably thought that was going to be the answer to any problems I might have had. But these things were not much discussed and the pressure wasn't intense because there wasn't the sense that you might, as it were, go the other way. I don't think my parents were worried about that because they didn't know about it.

I went to Glasgow University when I was seventeen and was signed on for an Honours English degree. I took French and various different history classes and political economy and Russian but English was the main thing. The fact that I took Russian was just because I had a close friend who was a Communist and was taking Russian for the political point of view. We were very close friends and I didn't want to miss him and so I went to the Russian class. He was completely straight but I was bowled over about him.

I was called up in 1940 and I registered first of all as a conscientious objector. They set up tribunals where you had to explain your case but before my tribunal had come up, I had changed my mind. It's difficult knowing exactly how these things happened but I think I felt it was wrong to stand aside from what was happening. It wasn't just simply a capitalist war that the worker wouldn't support. There was an actual enemy over there. I felt that I couldn't sustain my objection to killing but I suggested a compromise to the tribunal that I would be in the army but I wouldn't have a weapon and so I couldn't actually kill anyone. Shortly after that I was drafted into the Royal Army Medical Corps (RAMC) and after training near Peebles I was sent to the Middle East. I had the whole of the war there in Egypt, Lebanon, Palestine.

My main job throughout the war was Quartermaster's Clerk. The Quartermaster looks after all the stores, medical and non-medical, and I was his assistant. I was put into a big six hundred bed hospital unit – the Forty Second General Hospital. We got the casualties as they were passed down to us and we were usually quite a bit from the front. In Egypt at the time when the Germans under Rommel came right up to the gates of Alexandria, we thought then that the whole thing was going to blow up. Nothing actually happened to me and that was relatively rare. We got the results of the war, the casualties, but we were not in the midst of the fighting ourselves and that was even more true when the Unit was moved to Lebanon and Palestine.

There was both a lot of very intense friendship and actual sexual activity in the Army. There were always stories of the Air Force boys being up to that kind of thing but the Army was different was what I was told. A great deal of it went on and I'm sure it had something to do with the edge of the operation, the edge of life and death. You were on that edge all the time and the fact that it was often very difficult to find the time and space for sexual activity meant that it had all the more intensity when you did find that time and space. I was a private and you felt the officers must have known something about it but perhaps turned a blind eye unless it became really scandalous. I remember coming back from the nearest local town from a film show and it was late at night when the bus got back into the barracks. I was with one or two other people looking along the line of one of the other barracks and there were two soldiers in passionate embrace and no one said anything. I never found out who they were. There was a lot of that going on all the time and it had that mixture of something dangerous and at the same time liberating. Perhaps the very unexpectedness of it was liberating.

Contact was made in different ways. Sometimes it was just sitting beside someone on a bench and a knee would be pressed. Just a small physical nudge, a physical gesture would tell you that something was going on there. Perhaps nothing was spoken at all but you understood the message and you would perhaps talk to this person later on. At other times you might desire someone who wasn't going to be interested and you had to be careful. And there were lots of things in between and that was what I remember as being strange and, in a way, very interesting. There was one chap I remember, stocky, not tall, very fair, good-looking but in an extremely masculine way and very, very hairy. We used to go to the beach and you saw almost the whole body, at times the whole body, and I found this guy extremely attractive and fascinating. It was one of those things that never actually came to the bit but somehow both of us seemed to feel that it was OK not to take it any further. Sometimes we would go back together to the tented camp from having done something in the desert. There might be twenty men standing being pressed together, being jumbled together on the back of a lorry. I remember standing behind this guy, quite clearly pressed against him and he wasn't moving away and I almost came in that position. I was damp at the end of it. He didn't object but he didn't carry it any further. That kind of half-thing, half-relationship was quite common.

I kept up writing with my Communist friend from university. He was in the Artillery and we were both in Egypt. We might have met somewhere, Cairo or Alexandria. I wrote to him and poured out my feelings and he replied with a totally negative response. We both survived and went back to university to finish our degrees and the fact that he said he couldn't carry on with me on those terms meant that I myself had different feelings for him. I had two other particularly intense relationships during the war. One was physical, the other wasn't. The physical one was just something that went on from body to body but was very full and satisfying in that sense. The other one was really a pretty intense kind of love affair with a guy who was straight but liked my company. We were stationed in Sidon in Lebanon and we used to go for long walks into the hills. I really did like him tremendously. You have to have the physical thing and yet the non-physical thing which is love has to be there too. You are very lucky if you get the two coming together. It was always individuals that I remember. There were times when three or four people might know what was going on but there was no consciousness of any gay grouping or gay solidarity.

I think that more than anything else the dropping of the atom bomb on Japan hastened the end of the war and you couldn't exactly rejoice in that as an event in history. I enjoyed being back but I found it very hard to get into civilian life. It was difficult from the point of view of having rationing and all sorts of shortages for at least five years after the end of the war, but it was not just that, the whole war had made me terribly unsettled. I only went back to university because I couldn't think what to do. The fact that I hadn't been writing during the war gave me doubts about that too. There was relief at the end of the war but also a great deal of unhappiness in feeling that I wasn't adjusting to the end of the war, in peacetime terms at all. The war years had been very unproductive from the point of view of writing. There had been very good poets in the First World War who had written well about the most appalling scenes and I couldn't understand why I couldn't do the same. It was a five-year interruption in my writing, a five-year block. In the late Forties/early Fifties I was writing but not well. It was a bad time for me just because I felt I wasn't doing what I should be doing.

I got a good first at Glasgow and then there was one of those times when your life forks and you have to decide. I got the chance of a scholarship to Oxford to do a further degree or I could just go directly onto the teaching staff of the English department at Glasgow University. I chose the teaching job because I was twenty-seven and felt that I didn't really want to do any more studying. I did go down to Oxford and thought that I wouldn't be happy there. I decided then that I was probably going to stay in Scotland even if it meant I was missing the chance of a kind of mobile university career. I wanted a job that I could do and do well and I think it was also part of a feeling about Glasgow and Scotland that I perhaps didn't have before the war. Having been away from it for such a long time I had much stronger feelings about it when I came back. I liked the idea of staying there and committing myself to Scotland, just by living there and trying to make a good job of it. It took a while to become a good teacher but eventually I got to quite enjoy the job. I was also doing quite a lot of translation and translated the Old English poem, 'Beowulf'. I was taking up different languages – Italian, Spanish – and I made translations from poems in other languages. I got quite a few trips from the British Council to go to other countries to give poetry readings or lectures and I tried to learn some German before I went there. I enjoyed doing all that.

Homosexual activity was just something that happened as it happened. It wasn't something you saw as any kind of political activity. There were no clubs in the modern sense of the term. No papers or magazines. It was a very unorganised, scattered and spontaneous kind of scene. There were certain pubs you could go to that were known to attract gay people but they wouldn't want to be known as gay pubs. The best known one was in West Nile Street, not very far from the city centre, called the *Royal*. Some of the hotels had either a bar or a lounge. The *Central Hotel* at Central Station was a place that people often would go to. They might meet in a pub and go to the *Central Hotel* for a coffee afterwards. There was a certain rhythm in what people did without it being organised and you either fell in with it or you didn't. For a while I did fall into that kind of circle although I wasn't part of what you would call a grouping. Obviously there were parties. These hotels and pubs were totally mixed in a class sense. That's always been true of Glasgow and I think it's still true today. A place like the *Royal* would be mixed in the sense of not everyone who was there was gay but it was predominantly gay. There were lots of married men and that was surprising to me to begin with. It seems to be a very Glasgow thing. You're in the bisexual area before you know where you are. Lots of people who would hate to be called homosexual. It's very odd – protective self-delusion. Lots of people who are absolutely straight, but . . . with a big BUT at the end of the sentence.

I suppose I was just going around, feeling my way, taking part in this or that but not being very much committed until I met John Scott in 1962. I was to be very close to him for sixteen years. When I met him, this was a very absorbing kind of relationship and I didn't want to go back to the scene and didn't very much do so. It was both very physical and it was a love affair. It showed me that it could happen. All through the Fifties, I despaired that it would ever happen. All the physical things that happened then were very enjoyable but nevertheless they didn't lead to anything else. They didn't involve the feelings. It was only when I met him that there was this merging of the two. It changed my life in so many ways. My writing just took off from the time I met him and the great doubts I had about myself as a writer in the Fifties just disappeared and, touch wood, will never come back. I owe everything, in a sense, to that relationship.

He lived in Lanarkshire in a small village with a large family – a very close large family and so it was very difficult for him to break out of that. His job was there too and so we didn't actually live together. I saw him every weekend and we went on holidays together but we never lived together. I think also, as a writer, I always sensed, maybe subconsciously, that I had to be by myself to get writing. I find that if I'm with somebody in the same house or same room I can't write. I have to be alone to write. From that point of view also this relationship was always there but it left me free to do my writing. He accepted this too and it didn't worry him.

The 1960s was the period I enjoyed most – partly because of the love affair, partly because of other kinds of liberation. The new kinds of music that were appearing and changing attitudes towards sex and the new kinds of writing in America – the Beat Poets – and in Russia. The general feeling that it was a new phase beginning was very liberating. It may have come largely from what was happening to me in my personal life; it's hard to sort out the chicken and the egg in these situations but it was a period which I found very helpful, very enjoyable and there was happiness there. It was a very productive time and that, of course, makes you happy. For a writer, that's your whole job – to write. Anything else is secondary. So if you're writing, whatever else is happening in your life, that's good. The things that help you to write if you can identify them, you want to continue. If it's love or love of music or poetry or whatever it may be, if you can identify the sources of your happiness, you think long may these sources continue. The poems I wrote about John Scott were mostly positive poems because it was a very positive thing. I have written other poems about relationships which didn't have any happy outcome at all but the actual tension and frustration can lead to poetry as well. It seems to work both ways.

In the Sixties I was probably encouraged to write a bit more openly. It was a gradual process and I don't think there was any time you could see a sudden change. I did write some love poems in the Sixties that to anyone who was able to read between the lines were fairly open declarations. The one called 'Glasgow Green' which I wrote in 1963 was about homosexual activity in Glasgow Green late at night in the winter time. When I started writing that poem I felt it had to be written but I still couldn't do it really openly. The scene in the park is nightmarish and although you can't really work it out as other than homosexual, there's a sense of a mystery about it. I suppose that was the nearest I could get to being open in the early Sixties, long before gay lib. It was published eventually and nothing terrible happened and now you get it taught in schools.

It wasn't till the Seventies that I began thinking about the Middle East again. I think because it was so much in the news again. My memories were still very vivid and so I brought both the platonic man and the physical man into the poems thirty years after the events. These poems are in the sequence called *The New Divan*. The ones which are clear are the platonic ones; the one which is about the physical relationship is not so clear for it uses the word 'you' and that could be taken to be heterosexual.

We weren't politically active but John and I would talk about things when they were reported in the papers. We talked about the Gielgud case and Lord Montagu and Wildeblood and the distant possibility of a change in the law. The Gielgud thing I remember particularly because not long after Gielgud was charged one of his films was being shown at the Cosmo, what is now the Glasgow Film Theatre, and when his name appeared on the credits, there were hisses from the crowd and I thought – here's the intelligentsia's response to this poor man. I was never a great person for joining things and when the Scottish Homosexual Rights Group and so on were starting up I supported them but I never took an active part.

John and I went through all sorts of phases, great ups and downs, and I remember at one time when we weren't getting on too well and he wasn't seeing me that letters passed between him and my mother. Maybe she wrote first; maybe she saw I was unhappy in some way. She must have sensed it had something to do with this relationship and I think she may have written to him and said – why don't you two get together again? I didn't know about it until much later when he told me. I met his family and I think I was accepted. I never will know how much they knew about our relationship but they couldn't have avoided knowing it was a close relationship. When we went on holiday together they didn't raise any objection. They didn't talk about it; they just took it as one of those things. When he died I went to the funeral and his family gave me one of the cords to hold at the actual burial. I was surprised as it usually is only very close friends or family who are allowed to do this. They must have accepted then that I was to be given this position, which I was very glad to get. We'd had a bad quarrel a year before that and things weren't too good before his death. These are things you can't do anything about. I always regret it. The kind of quarrel that really comes out of nothing. Just blows up. Each person says things . . . really terrible things . . . you feel you'll never get back on an even keel again. Then the man dies and you can't say how sorry you were about it all. That was the one bad thing, bitter thing about that last year.

The poems I wrote about John Scott, all the love poems were very open to me but not, I suppose, to other people because the poems often don't give anything away. The lover is addressed as 'you' and not 'he' or 'she'. When it came to 1990, I was going to be seventy and I knew there would be lots of interviews coming up. I suppose it was fairly widely known that I was gay but, nevertheless, I had never properly declared the fact. I made up my mind I was going to be completely open and some of the poems of that time are perfectly straightforward in their declarations. That's a long time after the Sixties when I maybe should have been doing it but I felt I couldn't do it then. I don't think anyone really enjoys living with a secret life going on underneath and I don't at all regret having done it. There were no bad results of having done it. Schools seem to be able to accept it and I haven't been taken off the Higher English syllabus. The gay theme comes out now and again in different ways but it's not the central theme of all my writing and so people who are teaching the work in schools or colleges can refer to it without bringing in my gayness at all. Most of my writing is not coming from a gay writer as such but from a writer who happens to be gay.

I am writing different kinds of things these days. I wrote some poems about a visit to America and some poems for an anthology of city poems. The anthology has one poem which is much more directly outspoken than some of the ones I have done in the past. I took a few months to do a translation of *Cyrano de Bergerac* for Communicado. I like the theatre and I thought it was time to give us a Scottish version of *Cyrano*. The real Cyrano, the seventeenth-century one, was gay and there is a very interesting gay subtext to the whole play. I could imagine a production of the play which could be very different from the normal way of doing it.

As a writer I try to remain open to experiences as they happen and I think, living in a city, you store them up in your mind and you hope that they can get into a poem someday. One poem, called 'Christmas Eve', would be an example of that – just sitting next to somebody on a bus and being propositioned in such a way that it was impossible to carry anything forward. Little instances of that kind I've often brought into poems and they're nearly always based on things that have happened and I enjoy the idea of bringing little dramatic incidents into poetry. The poem called 'Head' – a punning title – is about an incident that did, in fact, happen but in poetry it's often quite difficult to bring in things directly. Glasgow is very interesting for a writer. The absence of a strong literary tradition in Glasgow meant that for a long time it was hard to write about the reality of things but it's possible now. Incidents which you know to be deplorable you store up in your mind and you may write about them in ways that you don't quite see at the moment. It's all grist to a writer's mill.

MOIRA DIXON

(b. 1922)

I was born near Dublin in 1922 and I came over to Scotland in 1967. I was part of a large family and there was always a lot of boys and girls milling about. My mates were playing with their dolls and saying, 'when I get married I'm going to have three or four children'. I never talked like that and I never seemed to accept that level of life. Perhaps the lesbianism trait was there all along but it didn't develop until I mixed with other peers and began to understand just what I needed, what I was seeking. I found out later there is a group in Dublin but I wouldn't have made the venture there because I had family commitments. My brothers were married and moved away. I was left with my grandmother and my mother and my sister and I was the breadwinner and I probably assumed the masculine role to be the provider and do the heavy work. I just did it and I got pleasure out of it. It was no bother to me to trim the hedges or clean the windows. That might have been satisfying the more masculine trait in my make-up. Everyone has both; it's just environments and situations that develop one side or the other. My family dwindled away until there was just myself and my handicapped sister left. She's not a bad case but she needs supervision and so I decided to come to Methil and live with my aunt because when she'd be retiring I'd be working. My aunt had been nursing here for forty years. I had been in the Red Cross for years and years and I always worked in the community atmosphere and so I gravitated towards nursing when I came to Scotland.

I didn't have much of a life at first. My aunt and I disagreed and so it was work and back home to my sister. It was the same type of situation – caring. I didn't get out as much as I would have liked and so I wrote a lot. All my life I always had women friends and in times of stress or strain or troubles there was always a woman there. There was always a woman there for back up, for interest, for sharing joys and pleasures. It was only when I actually came to Scotland that I took more of an interest in the gay scene and started to write to a girl in London that I heard about through the *Forum* magazine. We wrote back and forth for quite a long time but then come the spring holiday I was able to arrange with a female friend to care for my sister and I went down to London to meet this lassie. She introduced me to the gay scene and to lots of her friends and I just struck up, had a rapport with them immediately. I was fond of this girl and she was fond of me insofar as she was a war baby and she knew her mother was Irish. Over these two or three years she would come up to visit and bring her particular partner up and I would go down to visit her. I started getting *Gay News* and got in touch with a chap in Falkland. He happened to be in nursing as well and he had a group going and I started going there and keeping in touch. It was a mixed group – quite good. It was a social group and a discussion group and I became the treasurer for a couple of years.

I'd always had women friends but being intimate was never a part of it until I came to Scotland and joined different groups and saw and experienced different things and became fully aware of myself. I think I'm all the better for it because I know what I have to do and with all the ups and downs I know I can cope. To be a full person you have to know yourself. Back home I'd had some sexual intercourse with guys but it wasn't complete. I liked the guys and I liked the sensation of making love but outside of that I felt there was always something missing. When I had my first association with a female I knew exactly what that was.

I was also going into Edinburgh occasionally to a group in George Square. I met various members there and I met my partner, Margaret, there. She was in a similar situation to myself. She had a son of four years of age and couldn't very well hold down jobs; I had a job and my sister to care for. She has an Irish background and that made a link right away. We're both Catholics too. I used to meet her in Edinburgh and went out to stay with her parents when I could. She used to come over to me occasionally at weekends and I suggested coming to stay with me for a month. If we got on together we could see where it would go from there. She came over for a month and that was nineteen years ago.

I've been in nursing, as I said, most of my life. Some people were aware that I was a lesbian but I never shoved it down their throats. If they disagreed I just shrugged my shoulders and walked away. I got along with male patients as well as the female patients. The boys often used to think I was great fun because I was Irish and I was always ready for a laugh or a song. When I was working on a TB ward because I was good at communicating with them I was allocated the job of giving them their injections. When I appeared in the morning they used to say – here comes the darts player. I coped with them and, years later, when I met with them they would stop for a chat. Then I heard of an opening in a local small unit and I got a job there. Social welfare were able to fit me up, through my sister, with a house right across the road. I didn't have to travel into Kirkcaldy any longer and so what I lost in status I gained financially and timewise.

There was boys and girl students and occasionally something would come up about the gay scene. If they asked me a question I would answer it truthfully and if they were really seeking under-standing of a situation I was prepared to discuss it with them. I often met them outside of work for a drink or a meal. I think because they were students there were so many things they wanted to know, to understand and if I could help them understand the gay scene, my lifestyle and be accepted in a pleasant, normal fashion I was pre-pared to talk to them. Only once did the Nursing Officer mention it and she agreed that the patients had no difficulty relating to me. It was never mentioned again but the officers under her could sit and talk with me. My chum could come over to meet me when work was finished and we were accepted as a family unit. We were accepted as a pair by the older folk but they never ever commented. We went to all the dos, the nurses' weddings; if I got an invite it was for both of us.

Compared with my earlier years there's more openness with the young people. The younger people will be prepared to accept you, not as a sexual object, but as a person and you must be prepared to be as open with them. There are degrees of privacy where you won't communicate and where you shouldn't be expected to communi-cate. You don't walk into a heterosexual's house and say – what did you do in bed last night? Yet you will get some folk who will ask that question of us and I don't think they are entitled to an answer. There are periods of your life, moments of your life you don't share with others. They belong to you and your partner. Those that I have managed to reach in discussion accept that the homosexual is a sensitive, caring person. In general, more so than the heterosexual person because they're not living role images. They're living their own lives as a person. They're not putting on a front, a veneer – I'm macho, I'm a man, big and tough and strong. I would say the same for lesbians – you see yourself as a whole person. You don't have to be the ultra femme . . . hair, teeth and tits as the Yanks say. If you accept your own lifestyle and become fully part of it nobody can hurt you. There are a few tears here and there but they can't destroy you. I'm happy to be a lesbian and I've no dislike of anyone else who leads different lifestyles. More power to them if they are happy with it. After all, happiness is such a fleeting thing and you can't say you'll have it tomorrow. There's an old Irish saying that's very true – 'Yesterday is history, tomorrow may never be, today's the day'.

Our neighbours all know and we're invited around and about. If somebody asks us to something, I'll say that I have to check with Margaret to see if we're both free. The younger neighbours will talk to us as person to person and others are not so close but they accept us and stop for a gossip at the garden fence. I think one's own attitude colours other people's attitudes but then I have the capacity to communicate and because of my particular temperament and profession I've learned to control emotion. We had a bit of a problem when my friend's laddie was growing up. Other children started giving him a hard time and if we checked them for it they would stand out in the street and shout 'lemon' at us. We didn't let it get to us and for his sake we tried to keep it cool. He didn't mind it so much when he was young but at fifteen, sixteen he was becoming aware of his own sexuality and he started questioning. I was sitting by one day when he asked his mother what a homosexual was. We talked it over and encouraged him to be sure of his own feelings. I asked him if he would rather his mum and I split up and he said – no, because you're my mum too. He had a bit of a rough patch and we helped him over it as best as we could. We've had a good relationship with him insofar as he could discuss anything with us and we would be straightforward. He lives in Denver, Colorado now and when she was over for the wedding they got on their own to talk about the past. He said that he understood lots of things now that he was an adult that he hadn't understood when he was younger. He accepted that some people have a different way of life and he wasn't patronising. We were pleased because we'd tried to give him a good outlook on life and to help him to associate with other people and to accept that people are different and they're none the worse for that. We're pleased that he's turned out so well and we consider it a feather in our hat.

I remember back when I was the treasurer with the group in Falkland I tried to contact the local branch of Gingerbread because some of our branch had children and I felt they could use some help and understanding for the children's benefit. I contacted the Gingerbread group in Leven and they said it was a good idea but it came to nothing. They kept making appointments and not keeping them. I was straightforward with the woman I was dealing with but she wasn't straightforward with me. There's many a gay person has children and contact would help to broaden understanding between the groups. We might have been able to help each other with finance or outings or whatever. Eventually I got discouraged and just dropped it.

We've been together for nineteen years. How many marriages last nineteen years? If a couple prove that they have something special, a coupling, a unit, whatever you call it I can't see why it can't be as legal as any other mating. I can't understand what the heck the rest of the world is worrying about. It's just people being happy together and that's what life's supposed to be about. People being happy together and thereby cutting out aggression and wars and all the rest of it. It looks like going for utopia but if one doesn't try you certainly don't get there. My family accept Margaret as my partner and her family accepts me. I have a brother in Ireland and she has all her relatives in the States. We go back and forward and every summer two or three of them stay here. We have lassies that come, couples that come and stay the weekend too. There's a couple in Stirling, a couple in Bathgate, a couple in Dunfermline, a couple in Berwick. They'll get on the phone and say – haven't seen you in ages. I always feel interested in what is going on and that keeps you young.

I go to the meetings of the AD group in Edinburgh once a month. Most people say AD stands for anno domini. We're the twilight group, neither here nor there. We're not young enough to go dashing to all the discos and not old enough to sit at home and do knitting. We like to get together and have a meal, go to a couple of shows, visit each other. There's always ten or twelve of us but it varies. We have people from Stirling and Glasgow but they're not able to attend every meeting. And there's a hillwalking group too. We go to the club in Kirkcaldy that's run by Fife Friend on the last Friday of every month. When we can, we go because I can leave my sister for a few hours but I wouldn't leave her overnight. There's people we know locally too – bus drivers, shop assistants, clergy-men, a couple of doctors – and we know each other. There's a warmth, a support, just knowing they are there in the community.

I have accepted myself as a person perhaps because I had respon-sibilities early in life. I was thirteen years old when my only sister was born and it was accepted that she would be my responsibility after my parents died. I knew that one day I would have to care for her and have to provide for her and so I approached life with that caring attitude. Because I had little hassles along the way, I was more sure of my own capabilities and of myself as a person and of my ability to cope. I had no doubts of myself. I'm a person who likes to feel alive, who likes a challenge. I feel the need to be needed. I feel the need to live life to the full within my own field. And when you get along and find a partner to share in it, that's good.

JAMES MITCHELL

(b. 1927)

I was born in Bridgeton in Glasgow in 1927. We lived in a single end and then after about a year we moved up in the world to a room and a kitchen in Darnaway Street where my younger brother was born. By the time my sister was born, about a year and a half later, we had moved up in the world again to two rooms and a kitchen with bathroom. Those were the days when everybody knew everybody else and nobody moved. People went to local shops and didn't travel much outside their own area. I stayed in that house in Partick until September 1991 a year after my mum died. My dad was an engineer to trade and went to Canada during the depression. After a couple of years he came back over here and then married my mum. I remember as a kid I was told—if your dad had got work over there, you would have been born in Canada. But I had been born in this wee house in Bridgeton and I couldnae see how I could possibly be a Canadian. He became a window cleaner and my mum didn't work—those were the days when women's work was bringing up the kids. I left school at fourteen. At that time there was the Third Year Leaving Certificate and I missed it at my own school because I was a wee evacuee to Cumnock. When I got to Cumnock Academy they had already had theirs. So, having sat an exam at neither school, I applied to both places and got a Third Year Leaving Certificate from both of them.

I took pleural pneumonia when I was fourteen and then I started limping. Eventually it was diagnosed as TB and I went into hospital. I was in and out of hospital until I was twenty-five and in those eleven years I only worked for a year and a half. In those days the treatment was rest and fresh air. Too much fresh air, in fact. You spent a lot of your time out on the verandah and you slept out there as well. You wore jumpers, scarves, gloves and you had a tarpaulin over the bottom of your bed to keep the snow off. It was bloody cold; it was a terrible life. This was the cure – fresh air and hyperalimentation it was called. I remember writing a letter to somebody, it had taken me all day and a wee breeze got up and blew all the pages away. Heartbreaking. When I was at home, I was given a bed to myself because of my health and my dad had to double up with my brother. At one time the hospital tried to immobilize my leg to see if they could confine the disease to just the one bit of my body. My knee was in a splint and then it was in a plaster which came from my nipple right down to my toe on one side. It weighed two stone, that plaster. I was travelling to work on a train one day and the train gave a jolt and a soldier's pack with a tin hat on it fell on to my knee. So it was back into hospital for nine months.

I did some studying in hospital to get the preliminary exam to sit the insurance exam. I also studied Esperanto because I've always believed in internationalism. I was coming up to twenty-five and I'd only worked for a year and a half. When applying for jobs, I said—since leaving school at fourteen, I have only worked for one employer—and I'm still pleased with myself for thinking of it. One bloke who interviewed me was impressed with my honesty when he saw me and I got the job and that was the job I retired from. It was maybe a bad mistake on his part because I had an awful lot of time off and a lot of periods in hospital after that. But I was always very conscientious.

Even when I was on crutches I was still trawling the cottages. My body was in plaster but I was still trawling around. I had to be careful because people are noticed in these places and there's not that many people going in and out on crutches every ten minutes. I was probably about twelve or thirteen when I realised that I was different. I used to go to toilets to see men peeing to see what they had. There used to be a toilet at Partick Cross and I remember in there once a man showed it to me in the careful way that folk do in cottages. It was quite a long time before I realised that that was what he had done. I remember hoping after the first time I was picked up that I would meet the person again because I wouldn't find another one. I didn't realise the world is full of us. I never drank because of my medical history and I wasn't in a pub till I was in my twenties. I used to lead a quiet life, just going to the toilets and eventually to the pictures. The Tivoli Picture House was a unique place with four toilets in the stalls, one in each corner. Some gay men went there and you would live in hope that somebody would come and grope you. This was wartime and I used to keep my gas-mask with me and that came in handy if I didn't like them.

The fact that I never drank meant that I didn't know anything about gay bars and I never had the chance to meet anybody socially. You just used to meet in the toilet and have a quick toss off and away you go, end of story. You'd get to know the faces hanging around in the same places but you didn't get to know anybody. I used to go around with a straight guy for a long time. We met in hospital and we were both on crutches. We were well known because he was so much taller than I was. Because we were off work, I used to go on holiday with him and his parents and he would come on holiday with me and my parents. I remember once in Ayr he chatted up this pair of girls and I was absolutely terrified. It didn't come off but we were on the bus to go to their place.

I knew what I was doing with other men wasn't legal but I didn't think it was wrong. It was the old story that you can't have a crime without a victim. Having to do it up back closes seemed ridiculous and going through Kelvingrove Park at night was a problem, it was living dangerously. I canny remember the first book I read—it might have been *Quatrefoil*—but I had to keep it hidden from mummy and daddy. And my brother was a butch wee guy, a footballer.

The first gay pub I heard about was the *Strand* in Hope Street. I was going around with the straight guy at this time and we met an old school friend and arranged to meet in the *Strand*. We couldn't find the place and we didn't go but when I think back to it he must have assumed we were gay if he arranged to meet us in a gay bar. I was in my early twenties then and was so naïve. The *Strand* is where *Austin's* is now. There was also *Guys* on the corner of Hope Street and the *Royal Restaurant*. The *Restaurant* was quite a good pub. There was a little bar off the street and you used to go through to the back which was men only. There was a better class of chap there and you felt relaxed. I got to know people there as well though I've never been one to start up a conversation. The longer you stand there the more difficult it is. I always remember this big drip on the bar counter and it was going to stain this bloke's nice white raincoat and all I had to do to start a conversation was to tell him about the drip and I couldn't and I watched his coat getting all dirty and I felt so stupid.

I was a member of the Scottish Minorities Group in the Seventies. There was a place first in Sauchiehall Street where you went through a close and up a few stairs. Then they opened the Gay Centre in Queens Crescent. I always went on my own and nobody ever talked to me and I never talked to them. It was all very quiet and I didn't like it. I went to one or two SMG meetings but some of them got carried away—it was like a trades' union congress, re-drafting constitutions and that sort of thing. Even when you saw those people later in a bar they still didn't talk to you.

I met the man I now live with coming out of the toilets in Partick as I was going in. He said, 'does the 33 bus go this way?' or some stupid remark like that. I was thirty-six, walked with a limp and a loner and he was nineteen. That same week I was coming back from Edinburgh on the train and met this seventeen year-old bloke and fell in love with him as well. I was seeing the nineteen year-old one night and the seventeen year-old the other night. It was all very flattering with a seventeen year-old and a nineteen year-old after a man of thirty-six. Eventually it got to the point where I wasn't being fair to either of them and I had to make up my mind. It went on for about a month and I made up my mind and I never see the one who was seventeen then. He became a dentist.

Mum didn't take to him but I think the reason for that was that she knew he was keeping me from getting married. I always felt I wanted to tell her. I always felt she should know and yet it always used to surprise me the number of times she would say—look at these pansies on television. My sister and her husband were on holiday in Oban with their kids one time and we were up and stayed the weekend. That was something foreign to my nature to bring your boyfriend who is so much younger than you are up for the weekend. We've got on very well since. I never went to meet his mother. A nineteen year-old is not going to introduce his family to a dirty old man. She's a funny woman and I don't think she would approve. People have often assumed that we are father and son. My hair went grey when I was in my twenties. It used to be called the Dick Chandler look. People were paying to get their hair dyed the way mine was naturally. And I don't know why but I keep calling him son. It is embarrassing when you are asked if you are father and son but as you get older the margin is very different. A boy of nineteen and a man of thirty-six is a big gap but he is forty-eight and I'm sixty-five and that doesn't seem so big.

We've had our break-ups too. I once came home unexpectedly and found him with this other guy and I was shattered. This guy was being extra good to him but I went to visit the guy and told him that I loved my friend. We still get on each other's wick occasionally and get in a huff. We lead very different lives. Even when it comes to the time when we go to bed. He goes to bed early and gets up with the lark and thinks that the day has been wasted if he is not on the go by nine o'clock. Whereas I think there's something wrong with the clock if I waken before nine. I don't go to bed till one or two. He doesn't like going to bars but we used to meet every night, often in *Tennants* bar, before we lived together. There was no music and he liked the silence.

I lived with my mum until she died. I got on very well with my mum and I appreciated that it was not my house. She was always there to ask where you'd been and who you'd met and all that kind of thing. You had to be home where teatime was concerned whether she was cooking or, towards the end, I was cooking. If you were in at midnight, she'd say—I heard you coming in late last night. She wasn't nasty or nosey but she was housebound for the last five years and so nothing exciting was happening to her. My friend and I moved in together after my mother died. We'd been together for twenty-eight years and we'd been seeing each other everyday. I was going in for this operation and somebody had to look after me. My niece is a very modern girl and she encouraged us to live together. I've recovered well from the operation and I'm rehearsing for an amateur musical production. There's no whacking great numbers like 'I am what I am' but it's a bouncy show.

IONA MCGREGOR

(b. 1929)

I was born in 1929. It should have happened in Fife but I was a premature baby and I was born in England, near Aldershot. My mother was an Army schoolmistress and my father in the Army Education Corps. My mother had to stop working as soon as they were married. After my parents came back from the tropical climes which gave me my first memories, we lived for six months in Glasgow (Maryhill Barracks) and then in Perthshire. My father was an instructor at Queen Victoria School which is a military establishment. I believe it's gone upmarket now, but it certainly wasn't upmarket then. It was quite a rough place. We lived in the grounds of the school and I was surrounded by very tough little boys. I played with boys and identified with them rather than with my own sex. I didn't have much to do with girls except for my sisters and one or two friends to whom I was intensely attached. I wanted to be a boy and I was attracted to my female contemporaries from about the age of eight. When I was thirteen I was sent away to boarding school where I lived in an all-female environment. These erotic feelings towards my contemporaries bothered me a great deal. According to the wisdom of the time I was going through a phase, and I did feel desperately that I was a freak in not conforming to what other young women of my age were doing. When I reached my late teens I went out with men but I always felt awkward and disliked it intensely. The odd thing is that at my boarding school we used to speculate on what various pairs of teachers might be getting up to, but I made no connection with my own feelings. The younger you are, the less you can identify with your elders.

I went to Bristol University where I studied for a degree in combined honours – in my case languages and English. By that time I was aware of my real sexual desire for women but I didn't have much opportunity to do anything about it. I recognised that I was 'lesbian', but still had little idea what this meant in terms of life-style or sexual activity. There were no role models available, and it was some years before I got my hands on Dr Krafft-Ebing's most enlightening manual. At Bristol I had semi-affairs which became quite physically passionate with two fellow students. The first was with a woman who was certainly heterosexual and very much of a flirt. It sounds quaint now, but she was trying to preserve her virginity and didn't want to have sex with men until she was married. This was a common attitude in the late Forties. What we did never got below the Plimsoll Line, if I may put it like that. The other affair was with a slightly younger woman. She later converted to Roman Catholicism and although she didn't become a nun as she had intended, she immersed herself in convent life and I lost sight of her.

After Bristol I taught for a year in York and then I came to Edinburgh where I lived for a number of years. I pursued various heterosexual women who were flattered but not enough to succumb. I had very few women friends of my own age because as soon as they discovered I was lesbian they beetled off. One in particular was warned by a mutual acquaintance – I don't think you should be seen around so much with Iona; she is one of those, a lesbian. After that, she dropped me, although we had been close friends and I had no sexual interest in her. I found that heterosexual women either ran away because they found it rather scary, or they were intrigued and prepared to exploit the situation up to a certain point. I am talking of course about a different era. Things are much more relaxed nowadays between straight women and lesbians. During the Fifties most of my friends were gay men. Those were the days of camp – great fun. I enjoyed gay company and it relieved the sexual pressure I felt from heterosexual men. I also had some older women friends who were willing to discuss my problems and give advice. It was always – Go to London. You'll never get anywhere in Edinburgh.

At the end of the Fifties I did just that and lived for a year in Notting Hill. If only I'd known that gay people met at weekends in Lyons Tea House my life might have been entirely different! I heard about the Gateways and made my way there on one occasion. But I turned back at the door – I hadn't the nerve to ring the bell. The Gateways was a famous lesbian club in a Chelsea basement off the King's Road. It was where lesbians used to go in the butch/femme era. I actually did make my way inside it later on. I only touched on the fringes of the gay scene (although 'gay' was not a word in use then). Until the middle Sixties unisex dressing was unheard of. Women didn't wear trousers except for sport or riding or something like that and the distinction between the sexes was sharply defined. At the Gateways femmes wore frilly dresses and bouffant hairstyles and the butches sported suits, ties and Brylcreemed hair. Some of them would be holding down jobs as secretaries and wearing skirts and stockings in their working lives.

My own theory is that the butch/femme dichotomy sprang from a notion that homosexual women formed another sex. You find this assumption in *The Well of Loneliness* which is a terribly bad novel but interesting from a historical point of view. It implicitly supports the idea that lesbians are active masculine personalities who seek out other women as their lovers, while the latter are not real lesbians but normal women who have been seduced. In those self-oppressive days a woman who became aware of her homosexuality in the way I did would naturally identify with the male world, the active world from which she was shut out. Homosexuality wasn't seen as anything more than a pathological freak; the only role model available was the male/female one. Lesbian sexuality was not regarded as conferring an identity in its own right. The butch/femme divide was rigidly adhered to in the Fifties. You had to be one or the other; two butches couldn't get together, nor could two femmes. I don't know what I would have done if I'd managed to get into that world: in their terms I was androgynous.

After my year in London I went to work in Kent – to Canterbury. It was there I met a woman with whom I had a long-term relationship. This continued when we moved to the Greater London area. I spent seven years in Beckenham, but I didn't have any connection with the London scene such as it was. This was partly my own choice because of fears for my job as a teacher. One didn't want to be publicly recognised as lesbian then, when the social climate was so hostile and dismissive. You need to have lived through that time to understand the effects of it even on people who had a circle of gay friends and didn't suffer the extra pressure of isolation.

Towards the end of the Sixties the scene in London was beginning to open up for women. There was a magazine called *Arena Three* which later turned into the monthly, *Sappho*, run by Jackie Forster, and that flourished for several years. At about the same time my lover and I moved to Edinburgh, but our relationship ended a few years later. Her parents had never given up trying to separate us. She became involved with a man and left me. I still can't decide whether she was bisexual or just succumbed to unforgiving family pressure. We are still in touch but obviously not on the same terms.

My own parents were uncomfortable with my sexuality. I can't say there was any particular moment when I came out to them. It was a very gradual process. Whenever I tried to discuss my situation they wouldn't face up to it, but I was able to take this woman I've mentioned to their house and stay overnight. It was the same with other lovers afterwards. There was never any occasion when I was told not to darken their doors again. However, my mother had a strange attitude. She was very affectionate towards this first lover. When we left the house she would kiss her quite spontaneously, but when I went to say goodbye my mother would flinch and turn her face aside to make sure that I kissed her on the cheek. It was very hurtful. I used to wonder what on earth was going through her mind. After I became involved with the gay rights movement I once got myself into a very sticky situation and I went over to Fife to speak to my parents about the problem. They didn't want to know; they looked at me in absolute terror, silently begging me not to go on. They didn't even phone me later to ask if I'd managed to extricate myself. I can see it now from their point of view. In a way, I wish they had reacted more strongly and shown real prejudice. That would have been something to latch on to. But there was just this wall of silence.

I have two married sisters. The younger is unperturbed by my homosexuality. She is seven years younger than me, and has known since her late teens that I am gay. Our other sister is midway between us in age and like my parents has always dodged the question. Whenever I have introduced a partner she has accepted her on a purely social level, but never gone beyond that. She's never asked, How are you getting on with so-and-so, or I'm sorry you've broken up, or any discussion of that kind.

I became involved in the gay rights movement in Edinburgh in the early Seventies. The Scottish Minorities Group (SMG) started up in 1969. We met in a place called the Cobweb, which was the basement of the Roman Catholic chaplaincy in George Square. The first women's group was in Glasgow. We started off as four women and a transvestite man meeting in a Roman Catholic presbytery. There was strong opposition at that time from women's groups towards women working with men for gay rights. There were lesbians in these groups – in fact they formed the most active part of them – but separation was all the vogue then. I believed that the gay rights movement had to have men and women working together if we were to make any progress. I stopped working for SMG when the Broughton Street centre was opened up to homosexuals under eighteen. I saw this as a foolish move when there was (and still is) so much deliberate confusion between adult male homosexuality and paedophilia.

The SMG Women's Group was set up and ran in parallel with the befriending and other services. Eventually it met on a weekly basis for discussions and social activities. We drew in women from all parts of Scotland and produced a monthly newsletter called *Gayzette*. There is still a women's group attached to the centre but I haven't had contact with it since about 1980.

When I taught in England the question of my being lesbian never came up because there were still plenty of unmarried women in teaching. On my return to Edinburgh I worked first in Fife and then moved to an Edinburgh school which I mistakenly thought would be the equivalent of the girls' grammar schools I had known in England. It was a private school and the kind of place where sexual activity was never acknowledged – at least, not by the adults. Like all Edinburgh schools it was drawn from a much narrower social base than those I had known in England. Eventually the children began writing 'Miss McGregor is a lemon' on the walls. I took early retirement. I'm happy to say that I've been contacted by several lesbian ex-pupils and recently had a letter from one who wanted some information for her thesis on 'Scottish Lesbians in History'.

I think the most interesting development over recent years is our awareness of the very broad nature of homosexuality. Throughout the Seventies and most of the Eighties the fight was to establish the right of lesbians and gays to an open life style. We've suffered some reverses, but that is much more possible now and there's also a recognition that as many varieties of homosexuality exist as of heterosexuality. I heard Gore Vidal say on a TV programme that there was no such thing as homosexuality – there were only homosexual and heterosexual acts. When I heard him I thought – this is terrible! It's all very well for someone in his position. What is he doing to the rest of us? Then I realised that basically he's right. Minority cultures label themselves when forced to band into a tribe for protection. In an ideal world any form of consenting adult sexuality would be OK and we wouldn't need these categories. Of course, it's not like that, and I don't think it ever will be. Gays are too much of a threat to the insecurities of straight society.

I'm in my sixties now and as far as being able to relate to the issues that concern young people I feel I've passed my sell-by date. I'm still involved in the sense that I speak at meetings and write to the BBC and other media whenever I see anything that smacks of homophobia. I gave the gay movement a lot of time for almost ten years. I devote more time now to writing novels.

I sometimes feel that there are only three pensionable lesbians in Scotland, myself in Edinburgh and two others elsewhere. We are all attached to an organisation we call the AD Group. That's Anno Domini for the postman and Aged Dykes for the members. Baby dykes have a cheekier interpretation. I laughed when I heard it, but it's a pity that there's so much ageism among gay people – as much as among heterosexuals. I suppose it's the price we pay for climbing out of the ghetto. The AD group has twenty to thirty members who attend occasionally and about six on a regular basis. We meet only once a month but we socialise outside the meetings. We fixed the age of forty-five only as a benchmark – we have younger members. We felt it was around that time people's thoughts are beginning to turn towards the menopause, retirement and old age. There must be lots of over-sixty lesbians in Scotland but if you have grown up anywhere around the Central Belt those who have known you from childhood are very close at hand. It must be difficult to come out in those circumstances. I think it's a great shame if that holds anyone back. It's so liberating to feel you can be open about your homosexuality. I could never return to the closet.

ALAN ALEXANDER

(b. 1937)

I was born in Edinburgh in April 1937. My parents were middle class, both members of the Communist Party. The house always seemed to be full of minority groups – although I didn't realise that then – anything from coloured doctors or refugees from one regime or another. As a kid I had several uncles that were real uncles and several that we just called Uncle Bert or Uncle George and all, I discovered latterly, were gay. All multi-talented – played the piano, 'Red Sails in the Sunset', organised the Boys Brigade musicals for the church, all that. I had no concept of people being gay or being poofs or whatever the expression was because it was never used in the house. It was only at school that I heard other kids call my first English teacher a big jessie. He was just as nice and just as acceptable as Uncle Bert and Uncle Ernie because he wore a moss green cord jacket with yellow tie and matching yellow socks and suede shoes and it was only people like film stars on ocean liners who used to wear suede shoes. But the expression, jessie, didn't necessarily imply they were gay; my grandmother used it just like a big girl's blouse to say that somebody was just a big daft thing.

I was innumerate and dyslexic as a child. Even when I went to secondary school I couldn't write fast enough to pass most exams. I was brought up by my grandparents and their idea of doing things was to give children practical things to do. I was actually always very good with my hands. My grandfather was a tailor and so I could sew when I was quite young and my grandmother taught me to bake. I think it was because I couldn't sit and read books to entertain myself that they bought pencils and papers and colours and so I could sit for hours drawing, scribbling or doing practical things. And from early on I had a liking for gardening. There was this stuff called Glitterwax and I used to make things out of this wax. I remember making a big banquet with all this artificial fruit made from wax. And I converted the tea trolley into a little theatre and made wire puppets with costumes. I started taking pride in being able to do things like that. I was quite solitary and this was a way of asserting myself.

Once when I was fifteen or sixteen my parents went on holiday and when they came back discovered that the bathroom had been painted and alcove above the bath had a vase and a fake bar of soap painted into it. And I was expecting to get a hammering from my father for doing something as silly as that but that was what I wanted to do. I remember taking the little porch that they had and I painted the ceiling pale blue like the sky and then I painted silver and white leaves as if they were growing over the top of it. There weren't any decoration magazines like *House and Garden* coming into the house. I think that these were notions out of the films, things I'd seen in the movies.

I wanted to be elegant and loved things like photographic sessions but I hated being caught unawares. I was prepared to do studio portraits, well-rehearsed in every movement, every gesture. I think it's just part and parcel of me. It's something like a performance and if you were being watched you had to act your way through it – walking along Princes Street determined to look nothing other than determined. Once I started to do dance classes I loved it, took to it like a duck to water. While I was doing my art college training in Edinburgh I did virtually a full-time ballet training at the Scottish Ballet School as well. I went off on a scholarship to Stockholm and studied theatre design and ballet at the Opera House and I danced on stage there. I loved to shine and I always wanted to show off. But once done, forget it. And having done the dancing and having been on stage there was this sense of 'Oh, well, I've done that'. I was offered jobs in the theatre in Stockholm and in the Art college in Edinburgh. I'd never taught and it seemed too good to turn down.

I was a very late developer sexually. Other kids at school were really quite sexually aware at thirteen, fourteen, fifteen but I had no concept of what was going on. I also became something of a figure of ridicule because I had no hairs on my body and was singled out for that. I didn't have a happy relationship with other blokes and, therefore, no sexual contact. None of the mutual wanking because I couldn't join in; I'd watch others do it with a certain kind of admiration. When I first went to Art College at seventeen/eighteen my voice hadn't broken and I forced it down.

The first girlfriend I had was the librarian of the Art College. I was about twenty and she must have been twenty-three. I thought she was really quite old and she had it organised to get condoms and the whole business. I remember enjoying it all immensely and feeling that I was quite secure in that because I kept saying – was I all right? did I manage all right? And she said yes. I couldn't go into a shop and ask for condoms and I sent away to London for a box of one hundred and kept them amongst my dance kit. My mother emptied it out one day to wash my tights and found all these condoms. I think it was quite a relief but I had to answer to my parents why I had these. What were my intentions towards this girl? Was I going to get engaged? But then I moved on to other girlfriends. I felt quite secure until one of the male students came to visit me and threw his arms around me and kissed me.

I was really very disturbed because I hadn't been shocked by it. I quite welcomed it because it was the first person that had ever said – I love you, I love you – outside the sexual act. I started to have doubts and then I got a crush on one of my students. I was twenty-four and this was my first year of teaching. This boy kept turning up and wanting me to look at his work and he obviously had a crush on me. I thought I'd established myself as a heterosexual and that my past of being inadequate was behind me. I started having sex with the second boy and then I had a boyfriend and a girlfriend at the same time and I didn't feel I was having a complete relationship with one or the other. And then one started to ask you to jettison the other and it became very complicated. Once my parents had actually said to me – what about this girlfriend you've got? who's this boy who's always hanging around as well? I wished I was back in the state before twenty-one – never having done it. I was so buggered up about it myself, wondering why I couldn't make a decision one way or the other, that I went off to my father's doctor who was in the same lodge as my old man. It hadn't dawned on me, of course, that as a good Jewish doctor he thought it was a phase I was going through. He made an appointment for me to go to the Edinburgh Royal to see Dr Boyd. We sat and chatted and at the end of it, he said – I can see you think you've got problems but you seem well enough adjusted, you're fine. And I thought – if this is fine, something will resolve itself. And eventually it did.

My mother eventually loved the idea that I was gay because there were all sorts of spin offs for her. She had a continuation from all her old friends who had all passed on to their very cosy homes, low profile retirement really. For I produced all these terribly entertaining people from the ballet school and the theatre and my mother thought it was her youth again with all her gay chums. That gave her a kind of entree because she would go to the Abercromby Hotel and say – do you know my son? – and they did and that allowed her a kind of social life which was very nice for her.

Once in the Seventies my students set up a Gay Group and at the first meeting I went along to they were talking about coming out. I said I was surprised that there weren't more members of staff and there was a rather tight-lippedness about that. They said I shouldn't be mentioning names because these others might not want to come out and I said – what do you mean, not want to come out? I see them in gay bars. And then I remember I said to the boy who was leading the group – when did you tell your parents? When he said he hadn't told them, I said – why not? They love you. You love them. Is it important to tell the rest of the world you are gay, and not them? It was too painful in the first place to come out because I thought I'd disappointed my parents enough, being a dunderheid, and I didn't want to add to that having a gay son. At least that's how I imagined it would be. But, I said, once done and they weren't critical why the fuck should I be interested in anybody else being critical?

I used to go to *Paddy's Bar* in Rose Street with my mother at lunchtimes. She met all her chums there and my Aunty Bunty, who wasn't really my auntie – she was a furrier. I think it was acceptable for them to go into the public bar – because they didn't have a lounge or anything like that – because it was run by a woman, Alice Crossan. I don't think there ever seemed to be any fights or trouble in it and so maybe that had some kind of appeal. I think that I must have gone there for several years quite unaware there were gay people floating about. Then I started going there as a student in the evening and I suppose at that point I knew that there were gay people standing about in the bar, but I've no recollection of ever seeing anybody flashing or doing the loos or whatever. The most you might have got was a bit of a smile and if you were prepared to speak then you'd get caught up with them. They seemed to float between there and *Robertson's* on the next corner.

The change in the licensing laws during one of the Festivals when they extended the licenses to one in the morning to any bar that normally served food brought in people from the Festival Club and the theatres and then the place started to get the reputation that it was gay. And the *Kenilworth*, along the street, seemed to open up working on the same level – but I think it seemed a bit rougher and a bit younger. The other place, of course, was the Abercromby Hotel – it had the most wonderful bar. You came through circular doors and what had presumably been a drawing room, panelled with antique mirror glass, beautiful shantung curtains and the whole business – very much like David Mlinar. It was a bit like the *Rockingham* in London and would be full of blokes standing around in blazers. It still attracted heterosexual couples because it wasn't a place known for being rough.

If I had friends coming up from London I used to have a terrific fun time. I then had a studio flat in Raeburn Place and one of my ploys was to get Derek to bring his silver Daimler. We'd have a few drinks in the studio and then he'd take them quite a scenic route up through the New Town, along Forth Street and directly into Leith Walk. I would say – we'll go to the Imperial Hotel. You'd get up there and there was a big bow window thing, built right out onto a portico which overlooked Leith Walk. It was all fluorescent lights – like Piccadilly. I would take them there and there would be fifteen hookers and the place would be absolutely stinking of hairspray and beehives and as you walked across the carpet your feet actually stuck to the carpet because of the spillage and the chewing gum. In those days you could hardly ask for a gin and tonic. I can remember once dragging some people out into *Fairley's*, which was a huge, huge bar on different sunken floor levels, very popular with sailors. I remember Derek, with the camel coat over his shoulder, said – I'll get the drinks – and every head must have turned along the bar because obviously they thought that these queens went in there to pick up sailors. And he said to the barmaid – two pink gins, please – and she said – Ah'll gie ye gin but ah'm fucked if ah ken how tae mak them pink.

We'd go down to the *Eldorado* for the wrestling and then we would all slip back up for supper to the *Deep Sea Fish and Chip*. It was all communal tables and the loo opened directly into the dining room and you could sit there and see everybody going out and in and the whores would drag in whatever trick they had managed to grab. There was a subterranean lavvy outside – where the Catholic Church is – and the gay guys and the hookers all just used it, slipped downstairs and used the boxes. I think money more than likely passed hands from the hookers to the police and so if the hookers were safe dragging numbers into boxes, so were all the queens. I had quite a fascination for it because all the partitions were built of glazed bricks and you could actually lift whole bricks out and put them back in again. Whole arms and virtually heads could pass through and all the bricks were built up again as you flushed. I quite liked all the intrigue of it and the slightly theatrical daftness of the situation. It even got to the point where you recognised people by their shoes. I remember once in another loo in the bus station this wee foot tapping away and I thought – there's something about the scale. I put a note through and said – shouldn't we be in Evensong just now? Another note immediately came back – Ada, you bitch – she'd recognised by the content of the note that it had to be me.

I don't think people were stuck in those days for loos to go to because every block along Queen Street, for example, there was one of those French iron pissoirs and the same along Abercrombie Place. Two of them along Regent Terrace, Royal Terrace and the gardens at the bottom of London Road. It was very easy if you went into one and got a nod from somebody and they wandered a few blocks down and you thought – right, they're off. That was a situation the police could not monitor. They were knocked down in next to no time and then suddenly you ended up with only the one in the middle of Princes Street – the Carousel/Wheel of Fortune as it's called – Albert Street, a little one at the top of the stairs at Calton Hill and GHQ. One knew, as a kid, that you could go in the GHQ and see people wiggling their willies and maybe not be quite sure what they were doing but you could see an awful lot of that going on.

I remember when they had all those lightening strikes, the Three Day Week, and all of that, they used to advertise in the newspaper that certain sections of the town would be without electricity for x number of hours. Well, as soon as you realised that it was the section of town that contained Albert Street, everybody must have rushed there because they were standing there six deep in the pitch black. And the funny thing was that the police used to come crashing down but they'd put their torches on at the top of the stair and you could see the torches starting to shine on the way down. So everybody zipped up, standing looking as if they were drying their hands and the place absolutely jammed with people. I always was prepared to check out the newspaper and if it seemed to be a certain part of town like Corstorphine that was plunged into darkness there would be a row of cars outside some loo that was never used and it would be absolutely jammed with folk.

GHQ was downstairs and it was a long curve with about three dozen loos. From the first four at one end you couldn't see the four at the far end. It was politic and manners to leave the first few empty for folk who really just came down for a quick pee. There were two boxes at the far end but I don't think folk used them unless they were really foolish because there was only one way into the place and, if you were in the box, that could be you done. It was in the GHQ that I met Brian. I'd seen him before in the *Café Royal* just next to GHQ, where he worked behind the bar – this red-haired angel – I thought he looked like something from a pre-Raphaelite picture. He was trying to pick up a black man one night at GHQ and I was trying to pick up the same one but he took to his heels and Brian and I were left together. I don't think he'd quite realised what he'd got into.

His father, a company director, was the sweetest, most under-standing man you could ever come across and I think he'd known from the word go that Brian was gay. Brian introduced me as ten years younger than what I was when he introduced me to his mother and father – he was twenty-one at the time. The father very quickly invited me to everything. We were invited as a couple to family things and nobody dared comment about it. His father had an expectation that we would remain as a couple and we were together for eighteen years. After his father died, his mother lived here in one flat downstairs and my mother lived in the other. Brian and I separated for a couple of years, really in terms of him having a personal crisis and a lot of people said to him that he was living under my shadow and that he should see what it was like to live on his own. I don't know how he felt but I didn't think it was going to be an end situation and it didn't stop me going along to visit him and his mother. When he came back he announced to me that he was HIV Positive and had been for a few months prior to that.

The curious thing about him having been away for two years was that it allowed for a reassessment of how we felt about each other. We never had sex again, not because he was HIV Positive, but just because we'd moved into a different kind of relationship. We were much closer and these last four years were really the best. We wouldn't allow ourselves any contention or play games with each other. Towards the end he rejected all sort of medication and he wouldn't take any painkillers. I don't know if somehow in his own mind he'd managed to disassociate himself from discomfort and pain. When his father had cancer they had given him morphine which inhibits your breathing and you die quicker. He said – I'm in no hurry to die and I'll die in my own time – and he maintained that position until twelve hours before he died. Brian actually had nursed a mother who had multiple sclerosis since she was forty and had a kind of stoic approach to it. He had the same approach and he never said – why did it have to happen to me? People ask me if I'm thinking of having another affair but I think it's really quite difficult to see any other relationship in perspective if you've had four years of non-sex which seemed almost perfect.

I still have quite an active sex life; it's the classic thing – what I call DBT or Door Bell Trade. All the guys that I'm having relationships with are married but it means that they vanish and never get tangled in my hair. These blokes don't see themselves as being gay. One of them phoned up recently and said that he missed me. I burst out laughing and he was saying it as a joke but I thought that the day he said that and meant it would be a betrayal of his sense of his own heterosexuality. Another one, who is about about thirty-one, said to me – did you know I'm a daddy now? Life's terrific, he said, I've got her, the bairn and you. That's real Edinburgh – such a sense of life being complete.

Sometimes people will come into my house and say that it is fantastic or outrageous but I don't see it like that. I always wonder if they've been used to Morningside beige. The first thing for me is that the house is workable – nothing to do with the decor. It's part of my upbringing that nothing is ever allowed to get worn out or fall into disrepair. The garden's done, the drive weeded, the roans painted and so on. My mother, even when she became an alcoholic, always managed to run the house. Shirts were always ironed; meals were always there; the status quo was always maintained. And I still have a sense of that. I never felt I had anywhere to escape – this was it. I've always maintained the status quo in my home in the same way that my parents did and I feel immensely comfortable in it.

ALISTAIR ROSS

(b. 1938)

I was born in Edinburgh on November 9th, 1938. I was the third of four brothers. My father was a policeman and we suffered in a way because of that insofar as we were all kept on the straight and narrow. He was hard on us and we got physical beatings to keep us on the right track. I didn't get on with him all the time because of that but I got on fine with my mother and she tended to protect us when we got the beatings. She was religious and attended church and we were all brought up to go to church too. We were involved in the Sunday School and then the Cubs and the Scouts. I enjoyed these things and we were joining in with neighbours and friends from school; it was just part of the natural social process. It was a lower middle to working class community. A lot of people owned houses in the area but, equally, there was rented accommodation. It was a recognisable community with local shopping, a cinema and a cafe that we all went to as we got that wee bit older and could go out on our own.

I went to the local primary school and even then I participated in arty crafty drama kind of things that maybe showed my later orientation. I was in an opera company and drama groups in my immediate area and then I went on to larger ones in the city. I realised that I was gay when I was about twelve and I went looking for places where other gays met and drama groups fulfilled that function. My first experience was when I was twelve when I was being fitted for a suit in a gents outfitters in Edinburgh. I was taken into the changing room and fondled by the assistant. I couldn't honestly say now whether he was much older than me or not. I enjoyed it but obviously didn't say anything to my mother who was with me at the time. But, subconsciously at least, I started looking for similar enjoyment thereafter.

I found that enjoyment with pals at secondary school doing the normal thing, I suppose, at that age. One source of contacts was while I was in the Scouts and we went to learn swimming at Warrender Baths. We were warned at one of the early sessions of the possibility of – I can't remember now how it was put – being handled in the showers. So obviously I made a beeline for the showers. And I can't remember how I found out that toilets attracted gay people but there was one close by to the secondary school that I found worth visiting on a regular basis. Then when I was in my mid teens, I went down to Binns Corner in the town centre which was a great meeting place and was picked up there. I was paid the sum of six shillings for having sex with this older man.

He acted as a very valuable contact and introduced me to quite a number of other people, some of them I'm still in contact with. He took me back to his flat, which was quite a hive of activity. You were able to meet other people there and have sex. And having met up with other folk word gets around about where they go. It wasn't until I was in my twenties that I learned about places like Calton Hill and the pubs and the bars. I wasn't in a pub until I was twenty-one and that was *Paddy's Bar*. There were really just the two gay bars in Edinburgh at the time – *Paddy's* and the *Caravel*, which was attached to the North British Hotel. This is going back to the days before the licensing laws are as free as they are now and on a Sunday we used to go down to South Queensferry because you had to be a traveller to be able to drink on a Sunday.

I certainly had a very active sex life in my late teens/early twenties. Having accepted that I was gay from an early age, I wasn't unhappy about any aspect of being gay other than the fact that it had to be kept hidden. Apparently I was desirable and I had friends and I was involved in a wide range of interests and activities. Any affairs that I had never seemed to last more than twelve months – great while they lasted but dreadful when they came to an end. But I suppose I was sufficiently young and good looking that there didn't seem to be any problem in finding somebody else. I was very much in love with one chap but it wasn't reciprocated; we still indulged in sex but that didn't matter so much to me as to have his friendship. There were others, of course, and through one of the drama groups I was in I had an affair with this chap that I was in love with and it was reciprocated which was great.

I am diabetic and when I left school I found it difficult to get work because of that. I did eventually get a job in an office and once you've got a job it's easy to move onto another. I had several jobs dealing with money and finances but while I was at the Electricity Board I began to feel that what I was doing wasn't really where I wanted to go. I eventually decided that I would have to go and get further qualifications.

In my last job before I went to college I had a boss who had, as I learned later, interfered with boys in his early life. He let it be known that he knew I was gay because of mannerisms or affectations of mine. I was quite involved with him on a personal level but there was nothing sexual at all. He was being treated for alcoholism and he was not in the best of health or in the best of minds either. So he wrote to me saying that he would tell my father and he would tell the college that I was gay. That upset me considerably and eventually I spoke to my father about it and he dealt with the matter from you may say a semi-professional point of view. It cleared up a lot of matters and the threats never came to anything as he went away to London.

It was quite a dramatic stage in my life and it forced me to come out to my father. He indicated that he always suspected it anyway and his and my relationship improved in leaps and bounds. I didn't come out to anyone else in my family and whether or not my father said anything to my mother I do not know. I often thought that my mother must suspect as – well, mothers tend to. And there was an occasion later when I went out for a day or an evening with my parents and an affair of mine. That was the only time that happened and I often thought that situation must have made my mother realise.

I went on to a two year Youth and Community Service course at Moray House. I was a bit shy but it was very interesting and I thoroughly enjoyed the course. When I finished my first post was in Greenock. That was in 1967. Two years later I went to Kirkcaldy and then a few years after that to Central Region. I suppose there was a thought that I might meet similarly-minded people but that has not proved the case.

There was a much bigger demand on my time in the evenings when I went to work – sometimes four or five nights a week. There's no doubt that had an effect on my social life. I had to give up drama and music and singing. I found outlets for my sexuality in Turkish baths where I could find them. Being in Greenock, I gravitated to Glasgow – mostly at the weekends but then I often worked at weekends and so sometimes it had to be week nights. Baths and toilets were very much the only places for picking up people and that led on to sex in the first place. I would say the majority of my friendships with gay men have started off with sex; probably 90% of my gay friendships started that way.

I was one of the very early members of the Scottish Minorities Group (SMG) because I felt it would give more chances to meet other gay folk. I received their newsletters and went to the occasional meeting. When I moved into the Central Region I met up with one or two other members and in 1973 we started a Falkirk branch of SMG. We had monthly meetings with speakers and we went to different places so as not to be identified with any one particular meeting spot. We had social get-togethers as well as the formal, committee-type meetings. We had problems trying to advertise through the local press and so we really had to rely on personal contacts and the SMG Newsletter. I don't suppose we had more than twelve to fifteen members at any one time but the group functioned adequately and provided an opportunity to meet other gays. The numbers fluctuated depending on who was speaking and what was happening but it was a base for local people and I was able to make new friends.

We could certainly meet but it was very much a shrouded issue and there was always the concern that we'd be seen when we were meeting. Even when we had get-togethers in the pub – although there was nothing out of the way about a group of men in a pub – we'd be looking over our shoulders to see who was going to see us together. We managed to get a room in a school because we were trying to make the point about using a school in the way that other community groups did. We had three meetings there and then the let was cancelled but we didn't pursue it.

The group fell apart because the chairman and the secretary were an affair and when they split up there was nobody else willing to continue. I became the SMG contact for the local area and I did telephone counselling on an individual basis for some years. A chap from Stirling got in touch with me in 1982 and the group got going again. It wasn't an officially constituted group but we were trying to provide a service for, among others, young unemployed people. They were phoning up and saying that they couldn't afford to go to Edinburgh or Glasgow and all that we could suggest locally was a toilet or a sauna or the Turkish baths. So we got together and formed a group which has really gone on since then. It's fluctuated between as few as three and as many as twenty-one at a meeting. We met on a monthly basis over the winter period and we organised outings in the summer. We did attract a lot of young folk for a while but maybe they wanted a bit more activity than sitting in someone's house chatting over a glass of wine and crisps.

I almost settled down with somebody who joined our group. He travelled over from Kirkintilloch to the group and he and I had quite a close affair. He was quite a bit younger than me and he was one of those unusual people who preferred older men. I was about fifteen years older than him and he'd been used to men twenty years or more older than him. We got to the extent of looking at houses together but he chose to say that he didn't think there was going to be any future for us. I think we both sort of mutually agreed at the end of the day that it wasn't to be. He wanted to continue on a friendly basis and we had booked for a season of opera in Glasgow. We continued to go on a monthly basis but latterly I didn't look forward to that because it was so painful. I would say of all the affairs I had that was the most painful. Probably he was the one I loved the most. He moved away down South, back to Southampton, because his mother was unwell but he never returned any correspondence or anything. But I remember him with very great affection.

I don't go out to as many places as I used to but I go to the local sauna and there are times when I am fortunate enough to have sex. You find that a lot of the men that go there looking for sex are married. I think in this area, and it's probably reflected in smaller areas throughout the whole of the country, gay men felt that they had to get married through social pressure. Some of these married men think that just because you're gay you're going to give them HIV and yet they still want to have sex. I take no chances and the sex is all very safe. I go to the sauna in Stirling now since the old one in Alloa closed. It was like going into a club because it was 99.9% gay; I sometimes wonder where they all went to when the old baths closed.

I go along to meetings of the Lesbian and Gay Christian Movement (LGCM) in Glasgow and I have done for about five years. I'm quite resolved in my own mind that there is no conflict between being gay and being Christian. I am what God made me. But I know that many people in the Church would argue otherwise and I haven't come out in the Church. So it's nice at LGCM to meet people on the basis of being gay but also on the basis of being interested in religion and church life.

When I went there at first there was a ten-minute spot at the beginning – a wee service with a prayer, a hymn, a reading and somebody expounding a few words over the Bible. The chap who ran it then was a Church of Scotland minister but when he died that side of it tended to get lost. Over the last year, however, one of the university chaplains has begun to put on a ten minute service when he is there. At a recent meeting one of the lesbians did it and I was quite surprised because up till then we've relied on a minister. I like that because I felt we were lacking that aspect of being a Christian group. Once a year at Christmas we always join with QUEST, the Catholic equivalent, for a joint carol service. That's a nice social occasion when we all bring our own eats and share them.

I'm also very involved in my local church. I'm an elder, clerk of the congregational board and convener of the Flower Committee. I sing in the church choir and I edited the church newsletter for ten years. I certainly value my contacts with the church and the friends I've made through the church. One of them is gay but the majority are female. It's just part of my life and I suppose I'd be lost without it.

LENA WRIGHT

(b. 1940)

I was born in 1940 in Kelty. It was a tight-knit mining community about three miles from Cowdenbeath in Fife. I've only got one sister and she's younger than me. There's nae mines in Fife now but at one time there was five mines in Kelty. My dad wasnae a miner; he was a lorry driver and every school holiday I was away with him every day. He was a long-distance driver until I would be about eleven or twelve and then he just went locally. I went right through primary school in Kelty and then I sat the qualifying exam when I was eleven and went to a junior secondary school for girls in Cowdenbeath. They concentrated on commercial subjects for lassies. I first realised then among all the girls that I was different.

I kent I was different but what could you dae aboot it? There was nae publicity like you have now. I didnae ken what gay was; it was never talked about. There was one guy worked in the Co-operative and they said he was queer but I didnae ken what queer was. You heard them talking about this nancy boy but I never heard about anything else. And not a thing was mentioned about women. I had kisses and cuddles like a' the lassies but naebody kent anything aboot it.

I was wanting to join the police force and I got a job in a factory to keep me going till I was eighteen. But when I stopped growing it was impossible for me to go to the police and so I stayed in the factory. It was weaving and the only men that was there was the engineers, the guys that sorted the looms. The workforce was women. I wanted to be in female company. I didnae feel comfortable with men until I was older. The first woman I was with was when I was fifteen and I was working in a factory. It was all straight females but if ye seen somebody ye fancied ye just went for them. Maistly it was for a one-night stand but sometimes a relationship lasted two or three month. It was a' straight lassies. They a' got married and maist o' them are grannies now. When I look back it was really amazing.

I met them at work and we went tae the pictures or tae the dancing. I was always a tomboy and I dinnae ken if they realised how far it was sexually but it never made any difference. Where I worked there was girls came frae a' over Fife tae work; there was people fae Cardenden and Ballingry. If I said – mum, I'm going out wi' my pals the night, is it a' right if such and such stays? – she said aye. But at the same time you had to be discreet. You couldnae dae things like you can dae noo. There was no instruction manual to look at. It was a kiss and a cuddle and it led to other things. I was careful to make sure I knew them well enough and I never ever had any rejections.

When I was fifteen that's when rock'n'roll started. I was the first

Teddy girl in Kelty. My mother went mental. We had an old treadle sewing machine and I went and bought this pair o' troosers. They wer'nae drainpipe or anything but I sewed them up so they were skin tight and I couldnae get oot o' them. The guys had the drape jackets wi' the velvet collars. It was a fashion craze since it hadnae really been that long since everything was on the rations. We had an annual dance at the factory and I went wi' this guy Tony that I was friendly with – he wasnae gay or anything. We had been dancing and it was really warm and I says – what's that smell? I hoped you wouldnae smell it – he says. He ran out of Brylcreem and had to use margarine. It was rotten. Women used to Brylcreem their hair tae; they'd gie theirsel a DA at the back. They were great times – all live bands. But I kept everything separate and when I went oot wi' my pals to the dancing, it was to the dancing. The last bus from Cowdenbeath to Kelty was ten past eleven and the guys used to gie you a dance and walk you to the bus.

I went oot wi' guys as well and I even got engaged – trying to change myself. I was nineteen and all my pals were getting engaged and I just tried to conform. I liked the guy but there was never really any love. He was a miner and all his family was miners as well. Once during the Fife Fortnight, the Fair, his father was working and about five or six of us went doon the pit. It was quite an experience and I cut oot a bit of coal and brought it hame and washed it. The guy worked three shifts – day shift, back shift and night shift and I only seen him when he was on the day shift. I was aye glad when he was on the other shifts because I was away oot wi' the girls. I packed it in after about three years because I knew I would be leading him a life o' hell and I knew I would be leading a life o' hell myself trying to be something I'm not. I never tellt him why but my father said tae him – you're really wasting your time here.

I was in the Territorial Army for three or four years and I eventually went into the Women's Royal Air Corps – the WRAC. I had one serious relationship there. I was attached to the TA which was nearly a' civilians but I was a Regular Instructor. I was a corporal and because there was no quarters as such I got my own furnished flat for a wee while when I was in Perth. She was in the TA but she was in digs and so she came and lived wi' me. But it didnae work oot – too much personality friction. I was actually due to re-enlist but my dad wasnae very well and I didnae want to leave my mum on her own. He eventually died. So that was the biggest mistake of my life. However ye canny greet ower spilt milk.

When I come out o' the army I got a job with a credit firm. You got this wee van and you filled it full of stuff and went round the countryside selling it. They didnae have to pay, they just gie me ten percent and then I went back the next week and got another ten per cent. My round was North Fife and I quite enjoyed it. But they pressurised you into selling mair and I was selling stuff to folk that I kent damn fine they couldnae afford. So after five years I left and got a job as a machinist in a factory in Newburgh and from there I got a job emptying gas meters. Then I got a job with the taxis. Jack of all trades, master of none. I've been in this job ten years and that's the longest I've been in a job. There's one or two of our male drivers are gay as well but the majority o' them are straight. Naebody ever says anything except the ones that are gay and we have a wee bit yap.

When I was about thirty I had this girl as a friend and I says to her – Now, look, I'm gay and maybe you dinnae want tae go oot wi' me in case ye get tarred wi' the same brush. Oh tae hell – she says. She wisnae bothered. She was the first person I told. It's still there from when I was young to be discreet. You've really got to keep yersel' tae yersel' and be discreet and no say anything unless it's tae your really close friends, straights as well, they all ken. My sister never said a word but ye jist kent she didnae approve. My mum's dead now but I used to take her to gay pubs and she loved the gay crowd, especially the guys.

It's only about fifteen year ago since I was at my very first gay

disco. That was in Auchtertool in a hotel. From there we went to
Edinburgh. It was actually some gay guys from Dunfermline that
told us about the gay scene. We didnae ken anything aboot it. That's
when I got roped into SHRG – the Scottish Homosexual Rights
Group – and they had a Fife branch and a phoneline. It was for
anybody that wanted tae get in contact to talk about things. It's
difficult trying to talk to somebody on the phone and so we made
arrangements to meet them in a pub – the *Victoria Arms* in Kirkcaldy
High Street. It's no there anymair but it was a smashing pub. No
matter when ye went in there was always somebody ye kent. You
could sit at the bar and guaranteed somebody would come in and
you'd get a blether. We used tae go doon the street, dae your
shopping and land up in the pub. Sometimes it landed up in a session
and you came home wi' a' your frozen stuff thawin' oot. It wasnae a
predominantly gay pub but it was the pub we all went tae. There
was only one time that a guy came in and he was obnoxious and
started mouthing off at us but we managed to get him chucked out.

When somebody phoned up to the phoneline we used to meet
them at the *Victoria Arms* and gie them a wee bit of advice and tell
them where anything was going on. We used to have busloads to
different discos all over the place. There was a load of women come
up on holiday from England and they'd heard about the *Victoria Arms*
and they popped in. That's how I met the girl I'm stayin' wi' now.
One of the girls on the phoneline says – this lassie's coming through
from Methil and we're meeting her at the pub. There was a crowd
of us but it started from that night – fourteen year past August.

At that time she stayed wi' her gran. She lost her mum when she
was eighteen and her dad went away to Canada. She stayed with
her grandma until she died about nine year ago and then she moved
in wi' me. But before that she was here every weekend and some
nights tae. It's been great. Her sisters ken aboot us and they're great.
Before one o' them got married we used to go over and stay the night
and go to a gay pub and *Fire Island* and she would come with us

sometimes for the music. The other sister has got two wee boys and she goes over regular, once a month, to babysit and let them out. It took a long time for her dad to come round. He comes over on business from Canada every year and we never had any hassle from him but he just couldnae accept it. But he's alright now – after fourteen year.

When I first started going out with her we used to go out for a drink and then a kiss and cuddle in the car before I took her hame to her gran's. There was one time in the middle of winter when we went right along to the very end of Leven Beach. The next thing there was lights and I hear chap-chap on the windae. It was the polis and they told us to move on. The windaes were that steamed up I dinnae even think they kent it was two women. It's funny now but it wisnae funny at the time. That's the only time I ever had any trouble with the police.

It was hard sometimes leading a double life because you had a home life to think about wi' your mother and father and you had your ain life that ye wanted to go ahead wi' but you couldnae. And I had very tolerant parents. They never bothered me and my mum would never come into my room. I did a lot of socializing with straights and I had other relationships and you were keeping the both of them separate. There was one chap in Kelty that goes out of his way to look straight and it's no so long ago that I used to go to his works night out with him because he didnae want to go hissell. When I was in my thirties there was a guy I worked beside that took a fancy tae me. I had sex with him. I tried it to see what it was like but I wasn't impressed.

Where we stay is a wee close community – it's a part of Kirkcaldy but it's apart from Kirkcaldy. Maist o' them ken but naebody bothers us. I heard a couple o' wee laddies talking about it but, apart from that, there's never been anything. There's a nice wee local along the road that we go to but we dinnae really have much socializing here. For the past two or three year Fife Friend have run this disco every month at *Anthony's* in Kirkcaldy. It's amazing the amount of folk in Kirkcaldy and the surrounding districts that are gay. It's brill because it keeps you in touch. I'm getting too old for the bother of trailing away into Edinburgh and I enjoy meeting everybody at the disco.

I wouldnae really change what I had but they've got it a lot better now – laid on a plate. Newspapers that tells you where things are going on and I had to dae wi' the local *Palais*. People's attitudes were changing until the AIDS epidemic. I havnae had any hassle but AIDS has put us way back again for tolerance. It's no' just homosexuals but they get the blame for starting it. The drug addicts and bisexuals have a lot to dae wi' it as well, going home and infecting unsuspecting wives.

I've never had any problems. It would be worse if you were staying somewhere where you were going to get hassle. But no way would I show it. You dinnae mind the gay society, the gay discos and that where everybody's the same but I've been living a double life for too long to change now. I wouldnae move away fae Fife. I've never really considered it. All my friends are here and everything we need is here. We're here and we're accepted and we're happy.

LOUIS McPHAIL

I was born outside Stornoway during the Second World War; I don't remember any of it but I remember playing with gas-masks. At first I was growing up on my own; my brother was born five years later. It was fishing stock. My father, my grandfather, my great-grandfather – they were all herring fishing folk. The menfolk were away from Monday to Friday. They would come home in time for the harvest to start work on the croft. The women were beasts of burden. It was the women's work to do the heavy work and they did it all. The menfolk would stand by and light their pipes and lift the heavy creels of manure on to their wives' backs and take a seat until they came back to them. There were enormous families then. No family planning. My aunt had twelve or thirteen children and used to tie the leg of her youngest son to the kitchen table when she went off for a bag of peat which she did daily. That's all she could do, you see, tie him with a rope so that he couldn't get near the fire. She lived in a black house, but we lived in a white house. It was built in the 1890s but my father added an extension to it about 1950.

I remember the Sabbath being very drawn out and loneliness but during the week it was a lively place. People used to go out visiting until the wee small hours. You would hear a knock at the door about ten at night or the door would just open. The first thing they would do perhaps would be to take the batteries out of their torches and put them on the stool or by the side of the fire because batteries weren't so easily available and they thought that the heat of the stove or the fire would give some extra life. They would come in when their own work was done and they'd be with you until two or three in the morning. Now, sometimes, you would walk with them half way home and then you would stop at a crossroads blethering again. They discussed many things. They were all of the same ilk. They were all Free Church folk and there wasn't even a Church of Scotland person in sight. They used to talk about the Disruption of 1843 and they used to be very proud of the fact that they were descended from these people that made a stand against the Moderates of the day. The moderate ministers were the ones that were in cahoots with the landlords and what the landlord said the minister told from the pulpit. In my area, it was devastated in the last century. The people were driven away to Nova Scotia and to America and you can see the remains of their crofts to this day.

Gaelic was the language of the home and of the Church. I was eighteen years of age before I heard an English sermon. That was because the doctor's wife, she was an incomer and she had no Gaelic. They thought they'd better hold a service in English once a month for the poor woman. The organ is frowned upon. In our church there's no music or no hymns. Hymns in the home but not in public worship. So they got the precentor which is one man standing and reading using the old fashioned tunes. The Church was very strict. You couldn't even post a letter on Sunday or even write it for that matter. The preaching was evangelical, of a very fiery type. It was more or less repent now, and hell was very much in front of you. It disturbed you so much. They could be tender but that was very rare.

A very important thing is the respect we had for the elderly. My generation was the last to do that. If there were old folk we were happy and we were in awe of them because they had so much to tell us. The menfolk, they had never been to Barra or to the Southern Isles but they had been in Montevideo, South Georgia, New Zealand – they knew every bar in New Zealand but they had never been in the South of Harris. We loved the old folk. The Pakistanis on the island have put us to shame – they look after their old, but now we put ours in the County Hospital.

When someone died, a wake went on for three or four nights. They had to have an extended wake because most of the people were away on the mainland working, either in hotels or nursing or at sea. The wake was a feast. In the early days there was a fearful amount of drink and the Church had to step in because there was a fight at funerals. The bigger the size of the clay piggies or the jars the more they thought of the deceased. If you had perhaps two ten gallon jars then that was fantastic.

We were Gaelic people but we were forbidden to speak Gaelic in the school. The dominie, he had a special cane that he used for the Gaelic children if they spoke their own language in the classroom. They were indoctrinated to kill our language. To improve the natives. It would have to be English all the time. I remember when I was fifteen a teacher taking a radio into the classroom so that we could hear the Mod. Mods were Mods then. We thought it was heaven hearing our own language for the first time. We never dared to breathe, it was so exciting. If these teachers had taught us through the medium of Gaelic things like geometry or algebra we would have been delighted. They never told us about the Clearances – what happened on our own island.

Now the fairies. Every second hillock had to do with the fairies. We didn't call them the fairies at all. It was the gentle folk that we called them – the *daoine sith* – the peaceful folk. And woe betide you if you offended them. Before the evangelical Christianity that we have now, when the first cow calved, the first milk was given to the fairies because if you gave the first offering to them all would be well with you.

Every village had a seer or a person that was gifted. A burden but they had it. They could foresee things as clear as a bell. These kynochs, they believed in witchcraft. They believed that there were certain women that would leave their cow devoid of milk when it should have been giving a plentiful yield and the only way they could get rid of this was to wind the cow in red plaid and walk three times round it muttering an incantation. And whoever the witch was her spell was broken. If we saw an otter coming away from its usual habitat, coming near the houses, we knew that creature was trying to tell us something. It wasn't the supernatural but they were from their own world trying to warn us of something – fearful weather or storms – but it was looked upon as the gospel truth.

Of course, you knew the people so well, you could foretell things that were going to happen anyway. One of my close pals, he died before he was twenty-one, when he was twenty. When we were about fourteen, we started playing around with each other. We used to strip together and we would rub against each other. Mutual masturbation. We never kissed or anything. Nothing like that in those days. The only thing he used to say was – this is what brown hatters do. That's the first time I heard the term, brown hatters, and there was something about suede shoes too. In those days people who wore suede shoes were regarded as being rather effeminate. We used to ejaculate and that was that. Once it was over we went back to playing again. I can remember one or two cases where we did it in the open air and it was fantastic. But he was taken away at a very young age. We knew that he did not have long to live but he was a wonderful person altogether.

My first real experience was when I was about fifteen and a half. It was a first cousin of mine. He was twenty-one, a big handsome sailor, and he came into the house one night. He had had a few drinks but not drunk by any means. Dutch courage. My parents were away that weekend in Stornoway and after a while he said – would you like to touch this? He must have guessed that I had never seen a grown man's penis in my life – and it was a monster. He just said – come away to bed. And I did and he just entered me and I remember the pain. He was excited and, I think, a bit afraid of what he was doing because I was so young. He did it about twice. He stayed the night and I think he gave me a ten shilling note the next morning. Guilt. I felt it was wrong and yet after about three nights I was craving for it again. But he didn't corrupt me. Years afterwards we had proper sex together and it was very enjoyable. But then I started to work in Stornoway and the Church sort of – to masturbate was wrong. There was no guidance – nobody to tell you anything. I used to think that anything that happened amiss to me during the week was because I had thoughts of sex. I had this guilt about sex.

A strange thing was that there was a custom on the island – the wink of the eye – when young men used to go roaming the villages, go knocking at the windows of single girls and they would be let in. They went to bed and they used the withdrawal method and the parents fully approved. But if they were seen in the daylight walking to the post office or giving each other a kiss, that was scandalous and the girl was worse than a harlot. Whether they took that from Scandinavia or not I don't know. Now if you left a sheet on the line on a Sunday morning that was something to talk about. But to have a man in bed with your daughter, they were quite pleased.

Gay people existed; they called them bumbodacht. That was the derogatory term but it was used for people who were very open, degraded. But it happened on the fishing boats; the young lads had it off among themselves. Once they came home at the weekend it was never spoken about. But I heard my father and the other menfolk discuss it one night after a few pints. They used to talk about one of the galleyboys, a boy of fifteen, a cook. They used to bind him with a rope and one of them used to masturbate him. They hadn't a clue that the boy was into bondage, but there was always someone to give a helping hand.

I remember once when I couldn't get my *Daily Record* and I couldn't understand why. I was fifteen and there was a cartoon that I used to read every day. All of a sudden the blooming *Daily Records* were going on top of the larder. Right at the very top and I couldn't think why I couldn't see them. This day when my mother was out I stood on an enamel bread bin and I reached the very top and I took down the *Daily Record*. It was all about homosexuality – legal or illegal. It was the Wolfenden Report and it was my first contact with the word – homosexual.

I had lots of inward struggles between eighteen and twenty-six. I used to drink heavily because I wasn't finding satisfaction. Once I had a few drinks I had people around me but once the money gave up, I was on my own again. I didn't seem to attract people to me. I came to the mainland of Scotland when I thought I'd had enough. I met other like-minded people and the drinking ceased and the power of the Church seemed to lose its grip on me. I worked in hotels for three summers. I used to take the colour supplements from the Sunday newspapers up with me and profanely read them on the Sabbath. A turning point was an advert I saw for this gay liberation thing called the Gay Liberation Front. I was sure it was something to do with my lifestyle and I wrote and within a week they put me in touch with somebody in Edinburgh. Father John Breslaw from the Scottish Minorities Group wrote a lovely letter back and put me in touch with a male nurse and that was the start of a better life – or peace of mind anyway. His mother was from Lewis and he came down to see me and in 1970 we started the Scottish Minorities Group in Inverness.

We used to meet on the first Monday of every month in a Chinese restaurant and I've seen fourteen people turning up. All age groups from about seventeen to sixty-one. We used to go to somebody's house for a cup of tea. It was more or less instant sex. My gosh, it was lively. I've seen perhaps eight people – everybody at it. I was looking for my underpants one day and I found them on the leaf of my potted palm. I met a boy from Dundee who used to work in a pub in Fort William through one of these meetings and I spent a weekend with him in Corpach. The meal was good and the chat was good but we watched our ps and qs and other diners wouldn't have a clue.

We put an advert in the *Inverness Courier* – If you're gay, come one and all to the Rose Street Hall. There was an uproar. The *Press and Journal* took it up. One of our councillors – These perverts meeting and our youngsters playing table tennis. . . . they should have a room in the mental hospital. Then there were diehards coming with bricks and things and so we ceased meeting there. Then it was house meetings and it's been that way ever since.

I had been about three years in Inverness when I discovered cottaging quite by accident. I didn't know that there was such a thing took place. This guy said – I went down to the toilets and you know that young conductor on the bus . . . and I had guessed something was different about him. And he was one of the first people I met. When I took to the cottaging, I would go down at half past three and would stay there until two or three in the morning. When I went for the Church, I went for it hook, line and sinker; when I took to the drink I wasn't content with a couple of drams; it was the same with cottaging. It was sex, sex, sex. I've seen one night, five, one after the other – but emptiness at the end of it. I remember one young policeman – I knew him well – and I met him one night and he said – For God's sake, you're still not floating, go home to your own bed. Anyway, that all tapered off.

The faith that I discarded, it came back. My faith now is as strong as ever. I can cope with being gay. Like I could cope years ago with the fairies and the witchcraft and the hobgoblins – things that are not in the Bible. The people in the Church know about me and don't condone it, but accept me for what I am. There are others that are office bearers in the Church and they kid on. They would nod their heads when the minister was running down Sodomites and yet they're one themselves. But you find that, there's always the hypocrite. It's like the broth mixture we used to get. There was always in the broth mixture one or two black things that were neither barley nor peas. God knows what they were and if you put them in your mouth, they would always break your teeth, false or otherwise. Even among your own gay friends, there's always ones you cannot trust and others that might be a bit reckless with their own lives but as far as you're concerned they would never let you down.

A strange thing happened once I reached my late thirties and forties. I started to gather people around me, especially young people, and now at fifty there's always young people around me. I listen to their problems and they're not afraid of me. It's marvellous. There's one of them here that is very close to me. He used to cruise when he was about sixteen and I picked him up. We sort of matured together. He's twenty-five now, a good looking lad and he works in London. We're always in touch. He phones me nearly every night. We're not lovers anymore but there's a great bond between us and there always will be.

With the onset of AIDS, it's not the done thing to sleep around anymore. Cruising was fun too in my early days but now there's a rough element in Inverness; there's even a rough element in Stornoway. But I do a strange kind of cruising, cruising with a difference. In the summer months, the odd Saturday or Sunday morning when I come off duty, I go out between half past seven and a quarter past eight and if I don't get anybody in that three quarters of an hour, it's no use. There's always hikers that have arrived in the early hours and I have a way of chatting to them. I bring them up for a cup of tea and I never bother with sex but I give them some stories and put on Highland dress on myself or on them. Some of them stay with me the whole day; some of them stay overnight; I get letters from some of them. There's probably some of them have guessed and others haven't but I don't try anything. One of the things I enjoy doing with people now is massaging them and in the last two years I've started on people's feet – sort of reflexology. They relax with this and you're not taking advantage of their bodies but you're still in contact.

It's a long process. The seed was planted, perhaps it was always there. God himself planted that seed, I believe, and then it came above ground at puberty. The winds and the rain descended upon it and just like the good seed that is mentioned in the Word, it must have fallen on good ground because it nurtured. It's now part of my nature and I haven't rebelled against it at all. I've accepted it. It's grown into fruition and I believe that others are feeding off it – off that crop that was planted so long ago. They're feeding off me in some ways and I'm helping them as best as I can.

MARY AND JUNE

(b. 1942 and 1952)

Mary I was born in Stirling in 1942. I never knew my mother or my father and when I was about three months old I was shipped out to a children's home outside Helensburgh. They didn't like the idea of you being institutionalised and so they kept fostering me out. I had quite a few foster homes but my earliest memory of one was in Cambuslang when I was about five. After that it was Rutherglen, Tiree and all over. If only they'd left me where I was rather than the continual dragging out of one home and trying to place you in another. Most of the time the family didn't want you; they just wanted the money. There were happy times but, as a whole, my childhood was not all that happy.

June I was born in Lennoxtown in 1952. When I was five we emigrated to Canada and we stayed there until I was about eight. We were in a wee mining village called Virginiatown in Ontario. It was brilliant. One guy had a great big back garden and he used to freeze it over and we used it as an ice rink all winter. Our house had a wee bit of back garden and then it was straight up into the hills and into the forest. My mother was homesick and so we came back. I wasnae happy at first but I adapted. I'm an only child and that can be lonely especially if you are quiet and don't mix easily in the first place. There should be a law against only children. But I had quite a few friends till I was about ten or eleven and then it clicked that there was 'something different'. My aunt was saying something to me about when I got married and had a family of my own and I turned round and said I wasnae going to get married and I knew that I wasnae going to get married. I knew that when I was eleven and probably before that. I was attracted to girls but other girls of my age were going towards boys and I just could not see the attraction.

Mary I would be about eleven or ten when I felt there was a difference but I wasn't too sure what the difference was. I gravitated towards the girls but I didn't want to play girls' games. I wanted to play cowboys and Indians or Tarzan – 'Me Tarzan, you Jane.' I was about fourteen when I found out what the difference was and that was very harrowing. I don't know if it's any worse or easier when you don't have a family but being totally on your own at fifteen and having to get a job and someplace to live and you've got this on your mind is very difficult. You think that everybody'll know about you and see it on your face – like a big mark on your forehead. I thought I was the only lesbian in the world.

June I was twelve years old when I had my first kiss. There was a party at a relative's house and me and this lassie, a distant cousin, decided we would go out and play in the car. She was a year younger than me but five years more mature. Her sister was the chauffeur and we were being driven along to an imaginary place. I was sitting in the back with this lassie and we were talking away and she kept getting closer and closer and then, suddenly, she threw her arms round me and, vroom, a great big gummy and it was brilliant. I loved it. The sister hadn't a clue what was going on in the back. This went on for about two weeks and then she discovered boys and that was her. It was as if she had been experimenting.

I had a terrible time from the age of twelve to sixteen coming to terms with it. I was going out to dances and discos trying to do what was normal. There was one girl who was a good friend of mine for years and years and we had this what you couldn't call a lesbian relationship but it got pretty close to it. I think she was pretty unsure of herself. I came out to her on the night of my twenty-first birthday party. I was out of my skull when I told her I was gay and she went – Oh God – and just went away, the usual reaction. I told her that if she didn't want to get in touch that was fine but from that moment on she exploited it. The fact was that I was madly in love with her and would have done anything for her. If she was lonely and bored she'd phone up and say – let's go for a drink. There was one night she asked me to go back to her place and stay because her parents were away. That was like dangling a hook but on the way there a car with a fellie stopped and eventually she decided to go off with him for an hour. It hurt me so much that anybody could do that and that was the last time I saw her. That they could pretend that they had some feeling for you but in the space of three quarters of an hour they're away with somebody else and you're just left hanging there.

Mary The first affair I had with a woman ended up horrendously. I was nineteen or twenty and I was working in electronics in East Kilbride. It was the works' night out and I quaffed a few. I was in the Ladies when this woman, Irene came in. She was ten or twelve years older than me, had quite a few affairs under her belt and she'd been married and had a wee daughter. She was chatting away and saying – I'm really quite fond of you – and it suddenly clicked. The Ladies was empty and she took my hand and just wheeched me into the toilet and shut the door. At first it was just a wee gentle kiss on the front of the lips, in the middle. She looked at me and smiled and I looked at her and nodded and then it was the full blown kiss. It lasted for about a year and a half but she took me for odds dosh. I was in digs in Rutherglen and we'd go back there. It was a good-sized room and the wee wifey was half-deaf anyway and three quarters blind. But that first kiss was incredible, that much softer, much more pliable. Then she buggered off and got married.

I got engaged to a guy when I was in my early twenties. A lot of it stems from the fact that I had no family and when I went to the homes of friends who had families I was alright for a while but I always ended up feeling like a cuckoo. I thought to myself that the only way to get a family was to get married and create my own family. I got engaged and had sex but after about six months I had to give the guy back his engagement ring. I told him I was a lesbian and that was the ba' up on the slates because he was the cousin of a girl who I was very good friends with. If I stayed over at her place I used to even sleep in her bed. Just because you're a lesbian doesn't mean you are going to jump on your straight friends but she felt that way and cut me right off.

Irene had actually been my doorway to other gay women and I used to go out and have a few drinks with them. This was the mid to late Sixties and there wasn't a great deal on the scene, especially for women. There were gay pubs but I didn't find them for about another ten years and we went to ordinary straight pubs. I fell for one of these women and it wasn't until I went to live with her that I discovered she was an alcoholic. She was about twelve or thirteen years older than me and she'd been in the Army. She was a terrific person and she'd give you her last penny when sober but she was

completely the opposite when she was drinking. We moved to a flat
in Parkhead and I ended up paying for it and everything else because
her ladyship wouldn't work. Her family was brilliant but I think her
mother was frightened about what would happen to her if I left.
After three years I had to get away and her sisters agreed with me.
At one point I contemplated suicide and then I thought – why the
hell should I?

I wrote to Anna Raeburn, the agony aunt, and I got a lovely letter
back from her where she gave me lots of contacts and told me about
pubs like the *Duke of Wellington, Vintners*, the *Waterloo* and the *Strand*
in Hope Street. I persuaded her to go along to this gay group in
Kersland Street. It was run by a gay priest – a heck of a nice guy.
There were eight or nine females and about forty-nine guys. Anyway, she met another woman there, fell in love with her and went
to stay with her. We were about to be rehoused in Drumchapel and
I'd had the flat put in my name. So I moved to Drumchapel on my
own a fortnight before Christmas 1974 or 1975.

About half the people in the group were politically minded. I've
never been politically active but we used to go from there down to
the *Duke* and I got friendly with a couple of the boys. We thought
it would be a good idea to have a switchboard because at that time
Glasgow did not have any place for young gay men, young gay
women to get in contact. We had one heck of a carry on about
funding but we finally got it from, I think, Glasgow District Council.
We were at the top of a building at the bottom of Renfield Street
squidged between a Chinese restaurant and a gents' outfitters. There
were about nine or ten of us and I was the only female. We didn't
have any formal training or anything like that. When it started off
it was open on Tuesday and Friday evenings and Saturday and
Sunday during the day.

June   I found an advert for Gay Switchboard in the *Evening Times* one
day and I cut it out and kept it in my pocket for six months until I

had the courage to phone. After being let down by that woman I just locked myself away for about eighteen months. I didn't go anywhere apart from my work. The weekend when I phoned, my mother and father were away in Blackpool and I thought that if I didn't do something, I was going to be like this for the rest of my life – not doing anything, not going anywhere and being unhappy. I knew that I was going to have to do something if I was going to get out of this and so I phoned them up. It took me so long to pick up the receiver and another two hours to dial the number and then I stayed on the line for another hour. I arranged to go to their first meeting and when I found the place just up from the Clyde I walked round the block three times. It was fine when I got in but nobody was forthcoming with information about where you could go and socialise. Eventually I met a lassie called Shirley; to this day I don't think that was her proper name. We struck up a relationship and we started to go out. I was still at home and she was still at home and so it was difficult. We had nowhere to go and there used to be a great big billboard up from Dundas Street bus station that we'd nip behind. We'd go for a drink and later on if we wanted to have a bit of a kiss and cuddle we'd go there. I'm standing there in all this rubbish, this crap and I'm thinking – to hell with this. But we used to see each other regularly and it was wonderful the time she had to stay over with me in Lennoxtown when she missed the last bus. Eventually we found out that the best pub was the *Duke of Wellington* and on the first visit we met Kath and her friend. This was just before she'd decided to move out from Kath's. Shirley and I had to go back to Lennoxtown the next day for a rehearsal; she played the guitar and I played the drums. But we came back that night and Mary and I ended up playing cards. I think we became friends before we became anything else.

Mary We'd been in an affair for about three or four months and I broke it off with June because I felt we'd been pushed into it by the others and I don't like being pushed into anything. We went our separate ways and I started going out with one girl and June started going out with another girl.

June The lassie that I went out with had met Shirley and that was how we got in touch. I think I actually used her to a certain extent for my own purposes but I never told her any lies either. As our relationship went on I found myself returning here to Drumchapel because I knew what I wanted. All three of us used to go to discos and we used to come back to Mary's all the time. It was like a magnet. It was really strange. I would come here and we would sit and we would talk and we would sleep in the same bed and we would go to sleep. That went on for months and months. Some of our friends thought before Mary and I did that we would get back together again. But Mary had broken off the relationship and so there was no way I was going to make the first move.

Round that time the firm I was working for was moving from Anniesland to Drumchapel. It would take two or three buses and on the wage I was getting that wasn't possible. I was telling Mary that I'd need to give up my job when she said that I could rent her back bedroom. We decorated the room and then Mary was to be going up to Tiree for a week's holiday. We met for a drink in the *Duke* the night before she went away and she said that there was something that she wanted to talk to me about. But there was always something else going on and we never got round to talking about it. We came back here to Drumchapel and we were both drunk and we still never talked about it.

Mary We made it up that night.

June We never ever talked about it but actions speak louder than words. We had a rare time. After Mary had gone off to Tiree the other lassie came up and it was the most difficult thing in the world.

When I did tell her it was terrible. I've never seen anybody so upset. As it turned out the three of us still remained friends and she would come up here of a weekend and stay.

Mary She brought loads and loads of pizzas. Her mum worked in the pizza factory and every weekend she brought about fourteen pizzas.

June We were both working in those days and we used to go to a favourite Indian restaurant in a wee lane just down from Anderson Bus Station. The two of us used to go in there and get a curry for a fiver. There were always late night buses but if we didn't get a bus we would get a taxi. Transport out here is not that much bother, except on a Sunday.

We've never talked about it with my father but I'm sure he's sussed our relationship.

Mary Either he let it slip out or he told June's mother but when she found out she turned completely against me.

June We used to always go over to them at Christmas. We would stay over until Boxing Day. I phoned a couple of weeks before one Christmas and I said – We're looking forward to coming over at Christmas. She said – you're welcome to come but Mary isn't. When I asked why, she said – I don't know what it is but she's not welcome here. In that case, I said, I won't be over on Christmas Day. I got all the Christmas presents ready and it was about three or four days before Christmas and my dad had taken me to my Aunt Margaret's where there was a whole argument about it. I said – If you're trying to make me choose between coming over here or being with Mary you'll lose every time because she's got no family, she's got nobody she can go to and you're asking me to leave somebody here on their own. Later, my mother tried to calm us down but when I said – I'm no' coming on Christmas Day – she then said – Well, in that case, don't bother coming back. There was no contact for months but it was one of my cousins who brought it to a close when she had twins and I was a godmother. Now I go over on Boxing Day but I go over myself. But what's all this goodwill to all men? It's a horrible thing to ask anybody and I just wouldn't do it. My mum sees Mary every now and again but she won't come up here and I don't think there's anything I can do about it. It's sometimes like walking a tightrope. My mother wants to go somewhere and Mary's got plans for something else. It's very hard when you're trying to keep the peace between two camps, if you'll pardon the pun. She's stopped asking when I'm going to get married but as to the fact that I'm gay, I don't think she'll ever admit it or talk about it. I think my father knows but he tends to block it out. They're sometimes in a wee pretend world of their own. It is sad and strange as well.

Mary But you get problems with gay people as well. Just because a person is gay doesn't make them wonderful. A lot of gay people have this idea that because somebody is gay they're the best thing since sliced bread, but human nature doesn't work like that.

June We had a couple of girlfriends that we asked to a works' party for the firm that I worked for. Mary and I were going and we invited them to make up a foursome with us.

Mary They started kissing each other at the table. It was horrendous. You just don't do that to your friends. If they had been taking us to their works' do, we would never have done that. And they must have known the score.

June On the Monday morning I waited for my usual lift to work and it never came. When I got into work he said that he wouldnae be able to give me lifts anymore because he had to take his wife to work. I knew his wife didnae work and then the penny dropped. I got treated quite badly and got all the dirty jobs in the office. How many things can you do to a stationery cupboard? There were only two people in the office treated me the same way and that was the shop steward and Nora, one of the women in the same office as me. I'm still friendly with her today.

Mary I finished earlier at my work and so I used to come up and get June and I got abuse as well. I used to stand and take it and talk to them and nice them to death. It was terrible. She had six months of that and she was coming home here at night and breaking her heart.

June In the end I decided to take my redundancy money. But I just couldn't get a job. I was with the Job Club for eighteen months and I never got a job. I think the way I dress has got a lot to do with me not getting employed. I don't like wearing skirts of any sort and though I can look nice and smart in dress trousers and a jacket I will not wear a skirt to get a job.

Mary I was made redundant, about eight or nine years after June, in 1989. I thought we could start up on our own in business with the redundancy money. We went through quite a few ideas and we decided on babies and toddlers clothing. We did a business course and got the £40 weekly Enterprise Allowance. We thought at the time that the business course was the bees knees but those guys from the course don't live in the real world. Their advice was to get a shop and we did that over the back here in Drumchapel. With hindsight we know we did it the wrong way round. What we should have done was the outdoor markets or even some of the indoor markets and built up some capital. We started with the shop and fitted it all out but we found out very quickly that people here will not walk the length of here themselves. We started off Monday to

Saturday and then we decided to take Monday to Friday and take a stall at the Barras on Saturday. Then we met this chap and began to do the outdoor markets with him and halved the rent between us. We were making more money at the markets than we were in the shop. There was nae contest and so we gave up the shop. But of course we lost all £2000 of my redundancy money. Just as we were beginning to get into the markets and make a bit of money he decided he didn't want to do the markets anymore. Neither of us is drivers and so that was that hit on the head. We're not working now and so we can survive but we can't do a lot.

June   I'm OK if I can get some playing. I would like to think I could get some kind of band together, if not a ceilidh band.

Mary   We had an idea to start up a booking agency for bands. We tried to start that up last year but we put it aside until we could get some money together for advertising. I think it would be a good idea because it's nice being self-employed.

June   Once you've done it, it gives you the confidence to do it again. We do voluntary work with Wellwoman and the housing co-op.

Mary   We're happy living here in Drumchapel. Apparently Drumchapel is now being called Dykecity but I don't suppose that's why I'm quite content here. June and I have been together for sixteen years, sixteen good years, and that's the secret of our contentment. We get some kids calling us 'lesbie' but we just say – Yes, what of it? – and they're non-plussed because that's not the reaction they expected.

June   About 95% of the people in our wee area know about us. Everybody in this avenue. The people who work down in the hall know about us too and they don't bat an eyelid.

Mary   There was a ceilidh one night and June was doing her drumming. This woman that I always thought of as a wee toughnut was speaking to some other women and she says – I know that big lassie on the drums and don't you fuckin' say a word about her. I know she's a fuckin' lesbian but I don't give a fuck. I think that big lassie's wonderful and if anybody says a fuckin' word aboot that lassie, they'll fuckin' well answer to me.

June   When I first started coming up here we used to have parties and the place was stowed. There was always somebody who could play a guitar and you'd have a sing-song. Even a few years ago we had a big Halloween party up here. But now our own particular circle of friends has dwindled and dwindled until now they're just acquaintances. We havenae gone out for months.

Mary   There's a wee lassie across the avenue and she keeps asking us to go to *Bennett's* with her. She lives just across the road from us but it took her two years to tell us one night at a function down at the hall when she was half-drunk.

June   I think it was actually desperation because she didnae have anyone to talk to. Because although she told her sister, she needed . . .

Mary   . . . needed another gay person to talk to. No matter how good a straight person is they don't understand what you've gone through in the past.

JOHN SCOTT

(b. 1946)

I was born in Selkirk in 1946. I was an only child until I was eight and we lived with my grandfather and my mum and dad. I've got two sisters – one is eight years younger than me and the other eleven years younger. Although we were all in the one house, it was almost like two separate families. My grandad had his own room and I used to spend most of my time with him. It's no that I didnae get on with my mum and dad but they had my wee sisters and that kept them occupied. My dad worked in one of the mills in Selkirk and so he became stone deaf by the time he was in his mid-forties. I suppose it was a good thing that he was deaf because my mother talks all the time. We learned to switch off and you only actually heard anything you realised was important. Technically they were Presbyterians but they never pressured me even to go to Sunday School and I started going because you always got a book as a prize for perfect attendance. I never learned anything about religion but I had quite a good collection of books by the time I gave up. They were all members of the Selkirk Conservative and Unionist Association but that was mainly for the late drinking at the Tory club.

Basically I was always gay. As a kid, I wasn't fussy about playing kids' games; I was the one who stayed in and read books and played with my teddy bears. I was never interested in the wee lassies but when I was five there were two other lads and I liked to get their trousers down and have a look kind of thing. When I was nine we moved to another house and there was a thirteen year-old lad next door. He showed me how to wank and that lasted about three years till he got himself a girlfriend.

I was about twelve when I had my first adult male. This man – I used to think he was old but he would be in his thirties – picked me up at the Selkirk picture house. I cannae remember what the film was but it must have been really popular and by the time I got in there was only one seat left. It was next to this man and everybody knew he was like that. During the cartoons he kept trying to put his hand across but I pushed it away. Then he said – if you let me touch you I'll buy you an ice-cream at the interval. I was wearing a new pair of jeans and I couldnae get the zip down. So I went away to the toilet, pulled my zip down and came back and sat down beside him. There was folk sitting all round us but they just . . . like it wasn't happening. He bought me an ice-cream. I used to be in the Scouts and he lived right next to the Scout Hall. I used to go to the Scouts on a Friday and then climb into his bedroom. He was always there and I got past the stage of doing it for half a crown.

There was another bloke further up the road; he'd been in the Navy and I used to see him occasionally. Selkirk is as far away as you can get from the sea in Scotland but there were quite a few folk used to join the Navy. There was a bloke who was two years older than me who joined the Navy. I'd had nothing to do with him at school but I remember him coming back and he was wearing his Navy uniform and I thought – wow. He was a stocky bloke and what with the tight trousers, the Navy black and his gorgeous thighs . . . I managed to have it off with him in the pictures. We used to have it off when he was back on leave and although he's married now we still do on occasions.

I started working in the County Hotel on a part-time basis when I was about thirteen. I used to work in the kitchen or clean the bar. They started having dances in the ballroom on a Saturday night. Everybody knew everybody but one night a group of eight blokes came in – not local and dressed in the height of fashion. You were just beginning to get the start of Sixties fashion but in Selkirk the brightest thing anybody wore was a sports jacket. Everybody was watching them and when the jukebox came on during the band's break these blokes got up and danced themselves doing the Twist or the Shake. Folk thought they were shy and didn't want to ask lassies they didn't know. Then the band came back and played a slow number and they still danced. It was the first time I'd ever seen two men dancing together. Just unbelievable. Then they finished their drinks and went away and nobody had a clue who they were. It was the speak of Selkirk for weeks.

I left school at sixteen and went to work in Hawick. Hawick is twice the size of Selkirk, about twelve thousand. It always had a reputation and they used to say that if you dropped half-a-crown in Hawick you kept into the wall before you bent down to pick it up. There was a fairly open little gay community and they were all in the local operatic society. They were all as camp as knickers and, of course, I didnae like that but once you got to know some of them they were a good laugh. And there were toilets down next to the river that went like a fair – a lot of married men. The swimming pool was men only on Fridays from six to eight and after seven it was adults only. So it was always there . . . in the showers but it was very discreet. It was a terrible bus service back to Selkirk and so if I missed a bus I used to walk out to the edge of town and thumb a lift. A couple of lorry drivers picked me up and there were a couple of commercial travellers that I used to see quite regularly. One of them used to come into the bank where I worked and tell me no' to bother going for the bus at half past four, I used to go off with him and he parked the car in the quarry.

There was a lad I'd been at school with and we had an ongoing thing for a few years. We had the pretence of having girlfriends but I was never the least bit interested in being physical with them. When he left school he went straight into the Army. He used to come back if he was on leave and once he wrote and said he would pay for the hotel if I wanted to meet him in London. It was the first time down in the big city. We stayed in a hotel in Baker Street and that was the first time I was in a gay bar – the *Quebec*. We were getting fed drink there but we never took up any of the offers. I was still a small town boy.

At first the sex had been mutual masturbation. The young guy from the Navy was the first one to screw me and it hurt like hell the first time but I got to quite like it. The one who was in the Army started to like being screwed. I was doing most sexual activities but, funnily enough, I was never very keen on oral sex. It's much easier having sex with a man than going through all the hassle of chatting up a woman. The main thing was finding somewhere to do it. When the guy from the Navy came back to Selkirk he got a job with a van and we used to go to an old farm cottage three miles out of town. There were old mattresses and we used to make ourselves comfortable there. It was just sex but I saw him at least once a week, maybe twice. We used to go and see two blokes in their forties that lived quite close by. They were quite open about living together. Selkirk's a funny place because everybody speaks about everything but they dinnae really condemn anybody. We had a threesome with one of these blokes. That was the first time; it broadened my education a bit.

I was about eighteen or nineteen when I started going to *Paddy's Bar* in Rose Street in Edinburgh. I'd heard in Selkirk that that was where thae funny men go. I worked in the bank on Saturday mornings and I got the bus at half past twelve. In those days the pubs closed at half past two and after the bus got into St Andrews Square I was belting along Rose Street looking for this bar at a quarter past two. I got in, got a drink and just froze. When I came out I went into GHQ just by chance. I spent the rest of the afternoon there just looking. I went back to *Paddy's* and managed to get speaking to someone and then got the eight o'clock bus home. That was my first time in Edinburgh.

I soon got the hang of it all. I'd get off the bus at the Bridges and go into the *Café Royal* where there used to be some gays, have a pint and then go to GHQ. A couple of times I met somebody and we went up Calton Hill. In those days very few folk had flats; it was always digs that they got. I went back to Newington once with somebody and we were able to do it because his landlady was out at the bingo. And not so many folks had cars then. It was very much doing it in cottages but the only thing that worried me was getting caught. I never actually met anybody who'd been caught and they said that if you got lifted in GHQ you didnae even have to go to court; plead guilty by letter and get a £2 fine. So I felt a wee bit better about that.

I never really felt guilty about all this. I always felt that that was the thing for me and yet I was going through the pretence of having a girlfriend. Most of your nights out were with other blokes but everybody had to have a girlfriend. I started going out with a girl who worked in one of the other banks in town. She was nice and she didnae seem to bother that I wisnae trying anything. It was a convenient cover. We'd been going together for two years and it was assumed that we would get engaged on my 21st or hers. Instead of getting engaged, I emigrated. I wanted to have a change and Australian banks were advertising for bank staff to go over there. It was 1967 and a lot of Australians were getting called up to go and fight in Vietnam. So I got a job in a bank and went there on the £10 assisted passage scheme.

I was away for five years – first in Sydney, then Port Moresby in Papua New Guinea, back to Sydney, Port Moresby again and then South Africa. I would have liked to stay in Australia but while I was in South Africa they changed their immigration policy and although I'd been there before it didn't count as anything. I managed to find the cruising area in Sydney after a week and it didnae take long to find the gay scene. It was illegal there then too but the scene was very big. Port Moresby was a bit difficult because it was such a small place and you just couldnae get away with anything. But I managed two airline pilots and a commercial traveller. A lot of folk in the club were really homophobic and would be really bitter about anybody that they had their suspicions about. In Capetown there was one beach and one bar and the railway station was a big cruising area. There were lots of little cinemas where all the seats had trays in front of them. You could sit there having a meal and watching a film, while being groped by somebody as well. There was one picturesque square with Dutch gabled buildings where all the black female prostitutes hung out and near there were the black male prostitutes. They would do anything you wanted for twenty cents – it was a shame. One of my regular friends in Capetown was an Afrikaans policeman – big, heavy boned, heavy muscled, blond and he bred poodles. We used to go down to the beach with the poodles and he'd strip off and get screwed. The poodles were round about and so if anyone came near they would go – yap-yap, yap-yap. An early warning system.

When I came back to Scotland I moved to Edinburgh in November 1972 and started working in a bank. Within a couple of days I discovered the cottage in Albert Street and I bought a flat which was handy because it looked straight down on to the toilet on London Road. For a couple of years I had quite a serious friendship with a married man I met in the local pub. It just sort of petered out but we're still friends and he's still married. I must have this thing about married men. In 1979 I met a married man with three kids at the Infirmary Street baths – the poisoned dwarf. After about eighteen months of being his bit on the side, he left the wife and kids and moved in with me. It was actually Christmas that he moved in. He had keys for the flat. I was down at Selkirk for Christmas. On the Saturday after Christmas I was coming back and my mother wanted to go to the sales. The phone rang and he said – I've left my wife, I've got my luggage and I'm in your flat. So my mum and dad got presented with this at Christmas. They never said anything at the time but a few months later, when they were back up, he was still there and it was pretty obvious that only one bedroom was being used. They were very good about it. My mother likes him and she always makes him jam and sends him Christmas presents. All my dad ever said about it was in a pub one night – I dinnae mind that you live with a man, but does it have to be a Gala man?

We lived together for six years and I didn't do much at all but I cut down the cottaging. When he left his wife his kids were in their teens and they used to come down every Sunday for their tea. I'd be making their tea and although nothing was said to them, they're no' stupid kids and it was pretty obvious. Sometimes I gave them mince and tatties and doughballs and the youngest one thought they were really good. She'd gone back to her mother and said that she thought that my dumplings were a lot better than the ones she made and she'd like me to send her the recipe. I don't think that went down too well. We never had any hassle with either of the families. There was one time we went down for the Gala rugby sevens and we met his ex-wife and her boyfriend. It was quite a laugh because we all chatted away and I think everybody was disappointed there were no fireworks. I got moved down to Newcastle for eighteen months and we saw each other at weekends but when I came back we decided to have separate flats. After a couple of years it just faded; we never actually split up; there was never a big row or drama. He's one of my closest friends now and we get on quite well since that sex thing's no longer an issue.

Nowadays I go to straight bars probably more than I do to gay bars. I can go to a bar and look at someone I fancy and if he looks back, fair enough. But I cannot be bothered with the actual chatting up. I drink locally in the bars near Easter Road and everybody that knows me in there knows that I'm gay and nobody's ever said anything. The drink's cheaper there than it is in the gay bars. I used to go to *Fire Island* back in the early Eighties – a real mix of people, all age groups, all types. The building was in a pretty crappy state – if you stood in one place too long, you stuck to the carpet. And the ceiling fell in in the women's bar. The toilets used to go like a fair – sometimes there was more folk going to the loo than there was dancing. It was a bit of a miss when the place went because there's never been any other place to take its place.

It was back in the early Eighties too that AIDS began to get a lot of publicity. We were living as a couple at that time and he's paranoiac about health matters and so we were into safe sex right from the beginning. A friend of ours was one of the first folk to die and that brought it home very quickly. I go every three months and get the HIV test because I'd rather know and make sure that I wasn't passing it on. It's amazing the number of folk that would be happy to let you stick into them without anything on it because they say you look clean. It's very foolish.

I'm no' into chickens or young lads at all but I'm very friendly with a young lad of twenty-two. I knew him when he was nineteen and he was asking this, that and the other. I always said – if you ever screw, make sure there's a condom involved. I remember him phoning one time and saying – I've done it, I've done it, I've been screwed.

He said he'd used a condom but a couple of months later he said he was awfy bothered wi' piles. The cream that the doctor was giving him was not doing any good and he asked me to have a look. It wisnae piles, it was great bloody anal warts. That was the first time he's been screwed and the bloke gave him warts. I called him a stupid bugger. He went and got the test and he's no' let anybody screw him since. He's trying to limit himself to oral sex and mutual masturbation – but he's twenty-two. I think that the message hasnae got through to that generation. It's more folk in their thirties and forties who are bothering and there are some folk who are so paranoid they're using two condoms in case one bursts. I know two folk at the moment who have got AIDS and one o' them is twenty-six. What a waste!

I go down to Selkirk about half a dozen times a year now, for Christmas and the Common Riding. Most of the people I went to school with have left now apart from the guy that used to be in the Navy and the one that used to be in the Army. There's a straight guy there too that I've known all my life. If you'd met him when he was a teenager you'd have thought he was a screaming queen; he dyed his hair blond and wore Swedish clogs and was very theatrical for Selkirk. Everybody assumed he was gay and nobody thought I was. I was best man at his wedding and godfather to his son. A couple of years ago I went into the public toilet there and there were four married men in there and I'd been to bed with each one of them. I managed to introduce them but for most folk that stay down there it's just something they do on the side.

Some folk did try to set up a Borders Gay Group but it lasted a short while and then folded. Folk come up to Edinburgh for the gay bars and the numbers of people. Eventually, they'll either leave or end up in a marriage of convenience. Before I went to Australia, it was just assumed you would get engaged and married and that was it. That same pressure is still there for gay folk in Selkirk.

BRIAN McCROSSAN

(b. 1949)

I was born in Carluke in Lanarkshire in 1950. I was brought up in a council house and had seven brothers and one sister. Carluke was quite a small town, about eight thousand population, and so everybody knew everybody else. There had been mines there but they were closed by the time I was growing up and the economy of the town was based around the jam factory. Both my parents were Catholic and Catholicism was a very strong influence within the family. All the family went to Mass on Sundays and you were expected to attend other things relating to the Church. My childhood and schooldays were relatively happy. I had a lot of male and female friends and I tended to be someone who went out a lot in my teenage years. I was the second youngest in the family and a lot of the paths had been walked by my brothers before me; we were well known in the area and so it wasn't too difficult to establish a circle of friends.

I was aware by the time I was thirteen or fourteen that I was attracted to men. My problem then was about the strong feelings I had for school friends and the difficulties I had containing these so that I didn't end up doing things I would be embarrassed about. In fact, the kind of sexual contact that would have been regarded as normal between males at that age didn't happen because of my fears. When I was about fourteen a male, aged about fifty, who was known to my family, sexually interfered with me. Although I wasn't reluctant for it to happen it made me scared and I didn't follow it through with that person again. I kept quiet about it apart from telling a couple of my school friends and though we laughed it off and they gave me good support I didn't take any action against the man because I was confused about what I was doing. I wasn't sure if I was being led and also I did not want to have the embarrassment of talking to my parents and siblings about it.

My cynicism about Catholicism started when I was about fifteen and I had explained to a priest that I had masturbated. I was given a talking to and was then expected to say that I would never commit these sins again. I said that I would be committing these sins again and that if I said I wouldn't be I would be telling lies. He then said he could not provide absolution and told me to leave the Confessional box. I did go back to Communion again but that was my last time ever of going to Confession. This didn't stop me being sexually active but until my early twenties I felt guilty about the issue of confession and communion. My parents were bright, intelligent people but they were strong Catholics and although you could discuss social or political issues with them sex wasn't one of these issues. There was a discussion on abortion when I was fourteen/fifteen when I was going to be thrown out of the house and after that

I decided never to broach the topic of sex again with my parents. When I was about twenty or twenty-one I told my family that I was gay and that I was happy with it but that sort of discussion never took place with my mother. There was no problem about them knowing that I was gay and they were very supportive of me and that helped me throw away many of the vestiges of guilt. My mother knew I was having relationships with men but it was never discussed because I think that discussing it would have compromised her in relation to her religious views. Despite having a very good relationship with my mother this has always sadly been a gap between us.

In my teenage years I did a lot of socializing and I neglected my studies. I had no real plans about what to do when I left school but in those days, in the Sixties, you knew you would find employment somewhere. I picked up a *Daily Record* one day on the train to school and saw a job advertised for four months in a retail jewellers shop. Instead of getting off the train at Motherwell I went on to Glasgow and, still in my school uniform, I was interviewed for the job. They offered it to me and I was given a ticket to fly out to the Isle of Man two days later. I went home that night to tell my mother – my father was dead by then – that I had a job and was leaving home. It was not well received by my mother who said that it was the norm that you only left home to get married. I was clear that I wasn't going to get married and I knew it was necessary to leave home as soon as possible. She didn't want me to go but I had the ticket and I made it clear that we could either part on good terms or bad terms. We managed to part on good terms. One of the reasons for leaving home was to have the freedom to think about my sexuality and what my life might be about and I needed to escape from the family home to have some privacy for that.

I stayed on the Isle of Man in a very awful lodging house sharing a room with three other males. I was very homesick and it was very difficult to come to terms with that. It was the first time I had had to make new friends who were not people who knew me and my family. Making friendships had to be on a more open basis with my sexuality being part of it. It was very lonely and I hated where I was working but I required to do that to get the money and I couldn't go home either because I didn't want to lose face with family and friends. I don't think there was any sexual contact except for one episode in the last two weeks before I left. One of the males I shared a room with crawled into bed while I was asleep one night and tried to rape me. I did not wish his sexual advance, he was not somebody I had any interest in, he was somebody I actively disliked. We ended up having a fight and he was thrown out of the hotel the next morning. That left me with some guilt because if only we had talked about the sexual part of it at an earlier stage then it need not have got to the point of him attempting to force himself upon me. The job was a seasonal job and because I only got two out of the four Highers I sat I wasn't sure what I was going to be doing. I returned home at the end of October and decided to continue working for H. Samuels in Glasgow.

I moved into Glasgow after a couple of weeks living in Carluke. I was just over eighteen and very frustrated sexually but not knowing how or where to make it happen. One day at lunchtime I was in the book department of a shop in Argyle Street when I became aware that a man was watching me. He came up and whispered in my ear to go and look at a particular page in *The Gingerbread Man* by J.P. Donleavy. When I found the page there was a passage there about homosexuality and I blushed. He passed me a note and we met when I finished work that day. He took me to the YMCA building in Bothwell Street and he rented a room there for a few hours. That was my first contact of going to bed with somebody with that intention and it was quite a pleasant experience. It was full penetration and that was a shock but it was a relief that contact had been made. It did leave me feeling quite dirty because of the seediness of the joint and the furtiveness and the pain of the penetration. We met one more time and I decided that I didn't want to go back to the YMCA with him but we had a drink and we talked. He was about thirty-five and he was able to open up my education about gay bars and gay toilets and where you could meet. Soon I began to make my way around the gay bars in Glasgow.

Soon after that I had a relationship of about three or four months with someone who was about five years older than me. But he made a decision to get married and that finished our relationship. I was actually wanting to experience other people and in the latter part of our relationship I met someone whom I spent a night with in Edinburgh. He and I became close friends and that was the first friend I had on the gay scene. I then went on to have a relationship with an Australian who was living in Edinburgh. I wasn't sure about what I was doing workwise and then Samuels asked me to go up to Aberdeen. I lived in a caravan there and started to get involved in the Aberdeen gay scene. I was going out every night making contact and friends with people in gay bars. I remember one bar down by the docks which was very working-class and men from ships from all different countries would drink there, but at the same time it was a very open gay bar. In the beginning I would see the Australian every two or three weeks but that didn't last. I met a young guy from Inverness in that bar and though we never had sexual contact he became one of my closest and longest standing friends. I decided to move up to Inverness because I wanted to enjoy the Highlands and to move away from Aberdeen.

The next period of my life I wasn't thinking much about serious issues at all. It was a time of pleasure, going out and enjoying myself and not allowing myself to think too deeply about politics. But I was beginning to think that I didn't want to spend the rest of my life in H. Samuels. Initially, my life was very quiet with few opportunities to meet other gay men but I did meet someone in a laundromat after some four months. In Inverness only women went to the laundromat and men who did stood out. The second time I was in there another male came in and we got chatting and arranged to meet for a drink.

I was still living in shared accommodation and then, the first night I moved into a flat of my own, we slept together and that became quite a firm relationship. I had decided by this time that I was going to seek employment and train in social work. I also decided that, because the relationship was serious, I wouldn't leave to go to college but would stay and get some experience working within the mental health field; soon after I became a student psychiatric nurse. It was a shock to find that some people were more interested in containment than care. Despite enjoying much of the work I was doing and also my course work I reacted against the very restrictive regime that existed in the psychiatric hospital. I don't want to go into the details of what happened but the next two years were unbelievably unhappy. Physical threats were made against me because of the can of worms I was opening up and in the end I decided to go several months before my final exams. I was still in my relationship through all this and there were a lot of positive things but it was only when I left work that I realised I was on the verge of having a breakdown due to the pressure that I had been put under.

I went down to Edinburgh to stay with a friend for a few days and while I was there I went to meet Father Anthony Ross, the guru of the gay scene at the time. We talked and he helped me to understand the experience that I had just been through and to think critically about the confrontational way I had been using to deal with people. He suggested that I go to work in the Cyrenian hostel in Edinburgh and I worked there for nine months and it was a very gratifying and rewarding time. I was 'living in' and there were some very difficult situations and challenging dynamics that had to be faced. It was challenging and at times good fun and it helped me to build confidence in myself again. Leaving Inverness meant breaking up my relationship, although I wasn't consciously doing that, but I needed to be doing something challenging and the Cyrenians provided that. Anthony Ross also helped me to look at the sexual part of my life and to look at it in relation to the Catholic influence on it. He was able to talk to me about the Confessional and the fact that I hadn't been there since I was fourteen. It helped to put things into some perspective for me and I started going back to church again. There were other people who were homosexual going along to the church and so I could talk about it with them too. By the end of the nine months I had changed a lot. I did not want my relationship to continue but I did value his friendship and that was all quite hard. I also decided that I would go to college to do a degree in social work.

I started at Paisley in the autumn of 1974. Through friends I was introduced to someone who was renting a flat in the West End of Glasgow and there was a spare room in the flat. I moved in there in January of 1975. After about three months we started a relationship. He was about ten years older than me and we didn't intend to have a relationship but it just developed. We're still together and although we've had our ups and downs and for periods of time have lived apart we're still very much a couple and I find it a very satisfactory relationship. I've been promiscuous in my time but it's always been in the context of having firm and stable relationships. I haven't been very good at functioning without what I would consider a stable relationship.

The college life over the four years was fine. I took on part-time jobs and really enjoyed one working in the Theatre Royal. My sexuality was never an issue at college and I never talked particularly to my friends there about my private life. I felt very lucky that I came to terms very easily with my homosexuality and in my earlier thinking I felt that if I were accepted by my family then I didn't really care what other people thought. I didn't feel that I should have to explain my sexuality all the time, when people who were heterosexual didn't have to explain themselves. If people didn't like the fact that I was gay then they didn't need to come back and they would never be my friends. I was not involved with gay groups and until about ten years ago I didn't quite understand why people felt it important. I'm much more aware now of their importance and I can see the compromises I have made with people about the fact that I often wasn't able to talk about the pleasures that I got out of having a relationship with a man. I couldn't often talk to non-gay people openly about being in love. I recognise now that it is important to challenge the norms of our society so that people don't hold back about their sexuality and are not deprived of the right to talk about relationships.

I was still attending the Catholic Chaplaincy in Glasgow when I was at college and I was quite at ease with my sexuality in relation to the Church. It had been a liberal period for the Church. However, around 1976, I think, the Pope produced an encyclical letter against homosexuality and the priest who was reading it out was someone I had always regarded as supportive. Sitting there having to listen to this made me angry and I walked out of the church and never returned. It was a big step. I had often used religion as a crutch when things got bad. It was a test to see if I could survive, could face difficult situations without using religion and I realised in a short time that I could. It wasn't a clear-cut rejection of God; there was a period of two years when I still thought I believed in God although I wasn't actively thinking about religion. Religion was still very much part of the family scene and telling them that I no longer wished to be part of this was a second major hurdle with them. My friends had always seen me as a religious person and I think it came as a great shock to them that I could shed religion just like taking off a coat. Thinking about a life without believing in God, I believe, made me much more individually responsible for what I did with my life and how I conducted it. The future was not some afterlife but what I did here and now and what I passed on to other people was important. I developed my own personal thinking about love and about relationships and very positive things in life.

There were other issues that I was confronting now and that was about the social aspect and what people's lives were about. It was about poverty and the conditions that people lived in. I was starting to see all that on a more concrete basis than before. In my placements in the latter part of my course and once I started work in 1978 I saw all these issues on a daily basis and I was becoming more and more angry about what I was seeing. I had been political with a small 'p' through being in the Labour Party but I began to realise then that if I wanted to be serious about change I had to put it along side some sort of theory. On the day when Thatcher was elected in 1979 I was so upset that the Tories had won, even though I was dissatisfied with Labour, I made a very conscious decision that I had to become part of a group that was committed to political change. I didn't wish to face another election and feel as miserable as I did then because I had achieved so little in trying to change things in the activities I had been involved in up till that point.

I was by then actively involved in a union and had become a shop steward. There was a lot of infighting between Militant and the Socialist Workers Party at shop stewards' meetings and I found that, initially, a turn-off to politics. But I did begin to develop a belief that things would have to be changed by a revolution. So many horrible events were happening nationally and internationally that it would require much more than the innocent ways the Labour Party were going about things. It was my own long-standing involvement and my family's involvement with Labour that probably took me closer to Militant. In the early stages I'm not sure that I understood all the theory but by the time I actually joined Militant I didn't have any doubts that I was by then an atheist and moving towards being a Marxist. It has been an extremely valuable time for me since I joined Militant and it has developed me in lots of ways. It has had quite a lot of impact on my relationship because it's very difficult to be as politically active when your partner isn't as involved. There have been periods when we have separated; if you are spending a lot of time on politics, sometimes seven days a week, seven nights a week, you can't really conduct a relationship fairly.

In the last two or three years I've been less actively involved, not because of any political differences with Militant but as you become older it's difficult being out five or six nights a week doing a lot of the footslogging and being in a demanding job and doing my trade union work.

Being a Marxist has helped me to clear some of my thinking about sexual oppression and gay oppression. Militant as an organisation was extremely backward in relating to gay and lesbian issues when I joined. At first coming from the background that I did this was not the most important political point that I considered. However, the more I started to read and listen to people talking about sexual issues the more I realised there was a tremendous conservatism within Militant about homosexuality. Although Militant wasn't negative about homosexuals it was basically a tolerance as opposed to an acceptance or a sense of equality. When I first joined, their basic position was that after the revolution homosexuality would disappear because it was a disease of capitalism. Along with a few other Militant members I began to challenge this and to explain that one of the things I liked about myself was being homosexual and so their view of homosexuality wasn't exactly designed to keep me in Militant. Doing this kind of educational work was rewarding and I certainly believe that Militant have developed considerably since the time when I joined. It has helped too that other people have asked for a programme of gay and lesbian politics to be developed. It has also helped me to understand that it's not OK just to be comfortable with your own sexuality. Sexual oppression is part of capitalist society and it will require a revolution to change the basis for building a non-oppressive society.

The era of AIDS has affected me on a number of levels. I am much more cautious than I ever used to be about potential sexual contact. I had to be tested at an early stage when AIDS was starting to receive media attention because someone I'd had sexual relations with had died and had left a note with names of people to be contacted. I was particularly run down at that stage and, of course, I started to panic about some of the things I'd been suffering from. The three-week wait for those final results was very bad and looking at death in that way did have an effect afterwards. I tested negative. I had three friends die in a nine-month period in 1991 and they weren't people who had been particularly promiscuous; they had just been unlucky in their experience. To see people go through that sort of death is horrific. I think that the way the media has used AIDS has created a more backward attitude in society, even among groups of hetero-sexual people who in the past would have been supportive of homosexual lifestyles. I think the growing number of attacks on gay men can be linked to this hardening of the moral agenda. This process has been caused by the media's hysteria on AIDS but also more so by the hypocritical propaganda put about by the Tory government and the regressive legislation they have introduced which severely affects the lifestyles of lesbians and gay men.

I believe that the increased repression and oppression that lesbi-ans and gay men face now is also closely linked to the increased repression and oppression that is faced by many other sections of our society who have faced increased unemployment, decreased living standards and life opportunities as a result of policies pursued through the present government. This period has made me even more convinced of the need for a fundamental and revolutionary change in how our society is organised. Only then can we construct a society that frees individuals to live lifestyles that will be without the oppression and discrimination that lesbians and gay men have experienced up till now.

LESLEY NAPIER

(b. 1951)

I was born in Oban in 1951 and I spent the first seventeen years of my life there. I had one brother who was four years older than me. My father was a plumber and had his own business. He was a very quiet man and for the first few years I was very, very attached to him. Wherever he went, I went too – like a little lamb. We lived on a council estate and I had a very happy childhood. We had a lot of freedom and most of the time we were out in the woods, playing and running around. I suppose the main thing my mum was always drumming into us was no nonsense. It was straightforward and we never had any airs and graces about us. Both my parents had left school when they were fourteen, both were working class and they were quite keen that we make the most of ourselves. When I was ten, we moved to another house. We had an old auntie who was becoming quite frail and it was decided that we would move in with her and look after her. It was only about a ten-minute walk but it was a completely different environment. I felt separated off from my roots and all the people I knew on the council estate. It was different people, different values. There was parental pressure along the lines of 'would you like to go and play tennis with so and so?' I had been used to roaming around and I didn't have the airs and graces for things like playing tennis. For a couple of years it was a time of great upheaval.

There were times during my teenage years when I did feel a very definite attraction towards other women but I would never have said I was a lesbian. I had a very active heterosexual life in Oban and I was not at all interested in my friends sexually. When I was seventeen I promised myself three things – I was going to have some kind of a relationship with a woman; I would try out some drugs; I was going to become a famous artist. Until I left Oban at the age of eighteen, I never had any *desire* to form a sexual or emotional relationship with a woman. During my school years there were women at school who were lesbians. They didn't hide who they were and so they were always the butt of jokes. I just wasn't attracted to girls of the same age and I actually shared a bed with another lassie. But later on when I told my school friends that I was a lesbian they weren't tremendously surprised.

When I was seventeen I went to college in Carlisle. I was in digs in a big house and there were six of us girls in one room. It wasn't a big room – two sets of bunks and two single beds. I met up with one of the other girls in the room and we chatted. It just evolved. It was very difficult to have any kind of sexual relationship. You had to wait till everyone else was asleep and then jump into bed. But it was too quiet and, really, they were just waiting for us to get started. Some derogatory things were said and then I became aware that it wasn't something that was allowable at all. I think it came as a shock to me that I had to hide it. That was the most difficult thing. But I never thought that I had made a mistake. After the first time I just knew that this was right for me.

After Carlisle I moved on to art college in Liverpool. I didn't settle there. My lover had gone down to London and we came to the conclusion that one of us was going to have to move. Since London seemed to offer more possibilities in the long run I moved down and subsequently went to college there. The two of us did live together for a wee while and even after we had separate lovers, we stayed at the same address. We stayed friends. It was a very free time in the early Seventies and I moved around quite a wee bit. Battersea, Islington, Muswell Hill, Notting Hill Gate . . . Notting Hill was full of every kind of person you could think of. You could be anything and you could reinvent yourself everyday if you wanted to. We did smoke a lot of dope and dropped acid but I wouldn't say I was a hippy.

I got into the very serious lesbian feminist stuff then. One of the women I knew had got a fairly basic house through a housing association and she used to let the rooms out. I rented a room with her and then it seemed to evolve into this radical separatist thing, although there were two fellows there at first. I don't know how it evolved but it did. There were so many rules and regulations about who and why and all the ins and outs of politics. You had to be so accountable; it was worse than living at home. I remember this fellow turning up that I had gone out with. He hadn't been a serious boyfriend but he turned up on the doorstep and I didn't know what to do with him. I couldn't have asked him in. That would have caused a tremendous furore. So I was standing on the steps talking and I couldn't arrange to see him. It was like a closed order. You're cut off as a lesbian and you're cut off if you're a radical and it was an incredibly tiny group of people you were allowed to communicate with. Everybody else was taboo. I moved out because I got involved with somebody outside that house and when I moved it was like leaving the family all over again.

The woman I got involved with had five sons and so this was a big issue that I didn't know how to deal with. I hadn't had much experience of dealing with children, let alone dealing with five. But, in fact, I really enjoyed their company very, very much. They were all away at boarding school. Her husband was in the Army. But when they were on holiday they used to come and stay. Being with kids was a total revelation to me. But when I was much younger it was always the boys I hung around with and I suppose I was a bit of a tomboy. So being with these young lads was a bit like remembering a part of myself that had been totally forgotten. We'd go out for the day, go out hiking and I began to wonder what I'd been doing in London wasting my time. When I was around these five boys, my viewpoint began to turn round quite considerably and it opened up my life quite considerably. I'd done various jobs when I'd been in London – a darkroom assistant, developing photographs, photographs for posters. I'd been a minicab driver and a photographer. We advertised a twenty-four hour service – it was very shady. Men would phone up at three in the morning and ask us to go round and take photographs of them with their girlfriends. Or people would want photographs for stolen passports. I worked in a flower shop too and I was a barmaid. Then I began to wonder what on earth I was doing there in London and so I went up to Oban to work in the prawn factory. I worked on the pier and it was cold but it was great cracking prawns in freezing conditions. When I went back to London I realised that I hated the place and the people. I hated the whole culture. That's when we moved back up and got a cottage south of Oban.

She was a nurse and both of us worked in the psychiatric hospital in Lochgilphead. I left to work after a while in a papermaking place. Where we lived our neighbours were a couple with two wee girls. I suppose I had imagined that farm workers would be fussy about who they lived slap bang next door to but we had no problems about them giving us the cold shoulder and I appreciated that. There were a lot of lesbians coming up to see us, especially from Glasgow, but there were no problems. It was when I was living there that I decided I would like a child myself. The youngest of the five boys was six years old and I thought a large family situation would be good. As it turned out it didn't work out like that and we split up when my son was a year old. I enjoyed living there but economics dictated that we move. We moved to Edinburgh but there were a lot more people here and a lot more influences. Eventually we split up and she went off down to London with another woman and we sold the flat. It was pretty unpleasant because we were all involved in bringing up the boys.

I don't think it's a particularly bad thing to have one child in isolation but I'd never intended that and it does have its disadvantages. If it had been a girl I don't know how I would have felt if she hadn't been a lesbian but with a boy I feel that he can make up his own mind and not be so directly influenced by me. I think I feel that it is difficult bringing him up. He says now that he's definitely not gay but at fourteen I wouldn't have said I was gay either. It's difficult him trying to tell his friends about his mum and the woman I live with now. Boys are much more cutting, much more humorous and quite witty. They can give someone a hard time. If someone walks funny or if he thinks he can play football but can't, he has to take tremendous ribbing. I imagine that he has to take a lot of that as well because his mother is a lesbian.

My relationship with my family was always OK. When I got involved with a woman in the first place my mother was very upset and really anxious that I was going down the wrong track and that I would end up being lonely. Once they got over the initial shock my dad wrote me a lovely letter and it was very unusual for him to say anything. I'm sure they must have wondered where they had gone wrong but they never harangued me about it. When I told them I was pregnant my mum was, again, very upset about how I was going to support myself and bring the child up. Whereas my dad, straight off, was delighted. Once she got over that initial upset she reconciled herself and she's accepted that this is how it is. My extended family has been very supportive too – my aunts and so on. When I got pregnant I wrote to them all and told them that I was a lesbian and that I was pregnant and that if they wanted to harass anybody they should harass me and not my mother. What goes on in their minds I don't know but they accept the situation and I'm glad because that sense of belonging to a larger family is important to me. When my son was six or seven my auntie, the family dragon, asked him what he wanted to be when he grew up. He told her that he didn't know and that he might be a heterosexual or a homosexual or a bisexual; he just didn't know yet. That shut her up. Years ago I wasn't in contact with my family for a couple of years and I would never want to do that again. I think the important thing is that people accept what they see.

When he first went to school I was inclined to be honest with the school and tell them I was a lesbian but someone advised me not to do that because it would be stuck on his records to the end of his days. When my dad died he was six or seven and he found that very difficult and he was really acting up at school. The school kept saying that there must be something else but I knew that if they knew I was a lesbian they would hook everything on to that. He has had trouble with other boys hassling him in the street but there's been no problem from the school. The day he went to the high school his registry teacher was asking them about their families and when all the others had gone he went and told her that he lived with two women and that they were lesbians. She didn't fall backwards off her chair. Now on parents' evenings we both go with him to the school along with the mums and the dads and the nuclear families.

I'm self-employed and a lot of time is taken up with my job. I used to go round to lots of things but maybe because we are older there doesn't seem to be the same sort of zip and we all tend to be burrowing into our jobs. From my own experiences in the past I tend to veer away from close lesbian groups. I also don't feel the need to do particularly lesbian things. I'd rather do people-oriented things than have my sexuality be the factor that decides what I do. I like living in this part of Edinburgh too. It's a community and people are prepared to accept the small number of people who are not what they call average or normal. They're scattered but there are quite a few lesbian friends in these streets around here. It took a wee while for the neighbours here to accept us but now they're not stand-offish and they're not nosey. And I'm sure the woman downstairs has heard us shouting and bawling at each other.

I think it was only on leaving Scotland that I decided I was gay but I came back to Scotland and it was a definite choice because this was where I wanted to be. There are thousands of people in London and that makes it easier. But Scotland is important to me and whatever struggles may go on, whether its about AIDS or about gay rights, I'd rather be doing it here even though there's a lot fewer people around. It was easier for me in London but it was a positive choice to come back to Scotland because this is where my roots are.

Looking back on my life, I feel that I was thirty before I began to reappraise my life and make some long range plans. This was undoubtedly linked with meeting and becoming involved with Pat, my partner of twelve years now.

Although I knew I wanted my relationship with her to be monogamous, I was always afraid we wouldn't be able to weather all the sea-changes that that kind of relationship would involve. The fact that we have and that we ourselves have developed as people over the years is testament to our desire to make it happen rather than any supportive structure.

I know that it is very hard to live comfortably as a lesbian within a predominantly heterosexual culture, you feel doubly invisible both as a woman and a lesbian. However, if I could start my life over again I would still make the same choice, to be a lesbian because by and large, I am happy with my life. Contrary to what my mother warned would be my lot as a lesbian, I have had a very interesting life, full of love and adventure, so far, and I can safely predict that it will continue to be so, because there is no reason why it shouldn't be.

KUKUMO ROCKS

Growing up black in Scotland I wonder if we exist
We look in school history books but we dont exist
We buy plasters that are pink cause we dont exist
We buy toned spot cream thats white cause we dont exist
We look for black make up but it dont exist
We search TV screens papers in vain but we dont exist

On weddings and birthdays we look at smiling
White faces on cards cause we dont exist

On the birth of our children we see rose bud mothers
And pink chubby babies smiling up from rows of cards

We dont exist now
Our children dont exist
Growing up black in Britain
I wonder if we exist at all.[1]

I was born in Dundee. I have three brothers and one sister
and we're all quite similar in age. I was one when the family broke
up and I was brought up in an orphanage in Aberdeen until I was
ten. My father is West African and my mother is Indian. When I was
ten I moved to Fife to stay with my dad and I stayed with him until

I got married. It was a totally isolating and depressing experience growing up black in Scotland. When I was a teenager I used to say I was a Scot who happened to be black and when I was in my twenties I used to say I was a black woman who happened to be Scots. It's really difficult being black in a white society. My husband was white and I was the only black person in the town where we lived. It was very difficult being working-class too because I had no education and no one to discuss it with. I was so busy being poor and bringing up my children and trying to give them a sense of their black identity. Both children had asthma and they had it all the time. One of them was particularly ill with it and so it was a waste of time trying to get a job. I'd been dyslexic at school and so I didn't have any qualifications and I thought I'd end up working in a factory, which I did.

When I was thirty I started an Open University course. I did Sociology, Politics, Geography and Economics and I really loved it. I went on to a degree course at Edinburgh University after that. It was through them that I discovered I was dyslexic. I handed in an essay and I was encouraged to go to the dyslexic centre and that confirmed it. I studied Politics and Sociology and did courses on Gender and the Third World. I decided to look at the differences between black feminism and white feminism and I chose to do options about Race and the Law. I really think they should start looking at inequality issues and gender at primary school. They need to look at the kind of dolls and stories they get in nursery and primary education. The kind of images they have on posters should be thought about. They should definitely look at these issues in modern studies. In social work training, community education training, teacher training, where people have effects on other people's lives these issues should be thought about.

The first time I met lesbian women was when I was at university and I joined a group. It was something like 50% lesbians/50% straight women and it surprised me that they were normal just like

me. Then I became really interested to know about lesbian women
and I wasnae even thinking about it for myself at the time. I just
wanted to know. I suppose I must have been thinking about it but
it was never consciously so. Then my circle of friends became more
lesbian women than straight women. Around this time I met a
woman at university and we began having this close relationship.
I didn't put a name to it and in a way I didn't realise we were having
a lesbian relationship. There was a lot of holding back because we
were both terrified. In my final year I decided I had to leave home
even though I'd no money and nowhere to go. I knew some women
in a lesbian household and they knew that my situation was
desperate and I moved in with them. It was a bit of a shock moving
from a nuclear family straight into a lesbian household. We get
people down at the house shouting at us when we come out of
the house and that's part of the rejection that lesbians feel in
society.

   I'm still more conscious of being a black woman than a lesbian
woman but I don't know if that's because I've only been out a year
or two. To take on both would be very difficult. My own sense of
having a black identity only came in the 1980s when I started
reading Angela Davis and George Jackson. It's almost like I came
out as black and then in 1991 I came out as a lesbian. I became
more politically aware at university and began to understand the
inequality of women in general and related that to the inequalities
in my marriage. But university didn't do anything at all about
homosexuality. It's a big gamble to come out as a lesbian especially
if you end up being rejected. I told the people who mattered to me.
I told my sons and they were fine. As long as I was happy they were
happy. That was a big gamble because they were just at the age
when they wanted to be the same as everybody else and they might
not have taken it in but they were fine. The last people I told were
black friends because I had left Fife and moved to Edinburgh and
got to know black people and the fear of being isolated again was

terrible. But my black friends did accept me when I came out to them.

There's a lot of racism in Scotland even though people say it doesn't happen here. I've had two physical attacks recently and my son's been racially harassed. It seems to be growing. It's really bad in Glasgow and in Edinburgh there's a contingent of the British National Party and a couple of bases of the Ku Klux Klan. It makes me angry and that's why I'm involved in anti-racist work. Encouraging black women, enabling black women, going out to the colleges and universities and looking at the curriculum and trying to get things changed. White people do anti-racist training, think that's interesting and go home. I leave a conference and get attacked. In the area where I live everybody is white and I'm totally isolated there. It's really difficult to cope with. If you want recourse to black company, you've got to join black groups; that way you can make black friends. Sometimes there's a need for people to have a space they can call their own and speak about the pressures that they feel from a white society. Some white people ask why we need black groups and they forget that there are white groups everywhere. If you have a women's group you don't have men in it and it's not necessarily because you hate men, it's because you wouldn't want them there talking about women's issues. It's very difficult if you have to spend your time explaining to other people why you need your own space. If people are my friends and they want to find out about racism they should go and read books and then come back to me. It's got to the stage where I feel I ought to be a black separatist but that would be a huge jump to make.

I met another black woman at a conference in Glasgow and I was telling her how desperate my situation as a black lesbian was and out of that conversation the Black Lesbian Group was set up in the spring of 1992. There's only a few of us and we range in age from twenty to forty but it's been really great. We've been meeting on the first Thursdays of the month and we've been down to Leeds and

Manchester meeting black lesbians there. We discuss who we are and look at our histories. We'd like a black women's resource centre and space for a library and artistic activity and meetings too. We'd like the opportunity to get ourselves heard and be upfront and to be listened to.

Recently I've become involved in performing plays and poetry about black women. I sit back sometimes and I can't believe that three years ago I was a downtrodden battered wife. I wrote before I went to university and I was in a writers' group and we did the odd performance but it was really just amateur. I hadn't done anything for years but I'm involved in the Pan African Women's group and somebody asked me if I would do something for the African National Congress in Dundee. What I did was a celebration of black women, of our bodies, of our sexuality. I did it at International Women's Day and I dedicated it to women who love women and my supervisor was sitting there. It was videoed and a lot of people saw it and I was asked to go down to London to take part in a black lesbian cabaret. It was amazing – there were three hundred black lesbian women there. It's really taken off since then. I've been asked to do other things and somebody wants me to contribute to a book in Canada. I'm thinking that I could take up performing really seriously.

I'd like to see other Black Lesbian groups being set up in Scotland. I'd just like people to know that we exist. It's an educational process in a way, when black lesbians are seen to be around and doing things. If white people won't take on black issues then they're not going to take on black lesbian issues. But it's a problem in the lesbian community too because a lot of women don't think politically and aren't even aware of who we are or what our needs are. I want to see hundreds of black lesbians and I think the rest of the lesbian community could help us with benefits and crèches and so on. That would help black lesbians get the facilities they need. But in the meantime I am really enjoying being a black Scottish lesbian performance poet.

Who am I!
Who am I! I am a black woman of course!
Stand up, stand tall
Dig – ni – fied.

Be strong and proud
Cause your ass ain't peachy
It's like a dark plum
Your breasts ain't pink
But shades of brown
Nipples black as ebony
Be proud of what you got
Cause, baby, it's good
And it's hot.[2]

[1] *Growing Up Black In Scotland* by Kukumo Rocks
[2] *Black* by Kukumo Rocks

MAGGIE CHRISTIE

I moved up to Scotland to get away from a man. I haven't told this particular bit of my life story for a while – it doesn't feel so central to me now. During my 'separatist' days it did feel very central to my identity.

I was born and brought up in the south-east of England. I moved to Wales aged twenty-two and at the same time I became a feminist. It was pregnancy that woke me up to the oppression of women. Motherhood confirmed everything I learned about women's oppression in pregnancy, only more so.

By the time my daughter was one, I was beginning to realise I was a lesbian – or wonder if I was one – or decide to be one. A bit of all three really, and probably a few other variations too. I was confused then, but even now I find it hard to disentangle my realisation that I was falling in love with women, and had been for years, from my political realisation that the only sane choice for a feminist was to be a lesbian.

Meanwhile, despite managing to leave my daughter's father when she was nine months old, I had got into another disastrous relationship with a man, the third and last I lived with. I was isolated in many ways, despite having friends and being heavily involved in various political activities, both feminist and mixed (mainly anarchist and pacifist). I didn't think I knew any other lesbians where I lived until shortly before I left. Then I found out that two women I'd been in groups with for years were a lesbian couple – maybe everyone knew except me.

I travelled around a lot to conferences, especially ones with crèches. Feminist conferences did tend to have a higher crèche count than most others.

At an anarcha-feminist conference in Manchester in 1978 I bought some copies of the *Tayside Women's Liberation Newsletter* and the *St Andrews Lesbian-Feminist Newsletter*. (St Andrews was the centre of the radical feminist universe!) When I read them I knew this – radical feminism – was the politics I had been looking for. It was all so wonderfully clear. Women's oppression was men's fault. It made sense for women to get out of heterosexual relationships and be lesbians. I'd been struggling with these ideas on my own and here were women who seemed to have them all worked out.

I knew I had to meet these women. I contrived to do so at a Radical and Revolutionary Feminist conference in Brighton that autumn. After that we wrote letters. Meanwhile, I started a women-only newsletter, got into a lot of debilitating arguments with socialist feminists, and felt as if I was living a double life, not to say going crazy. My relationship with the man I was living with was awful. I don't know what he was getting out of it, but I was getting a place to live. My attempts to find somewhere to move out to, with a small child, came to nothing.

In January 1979 I went to London for a Reclaim the Night March. The organisers had called for national support following one on which a lot of women had been arrested and beaten up by the police. There was a huge feeling of a supportive 'all-everywhere' feminist community. We all seemed to know each other, or to be prepared to know each other, and really to be united.

After the march I went straight on in the coach women from Edinburgh had organised, and on up to Fife with K, one of the 'Tayside WLN writers', whom I was getting somewhat attached to. My daughter was staying with my mother and my brother (presumably my father was there too, though hardly likely to be doing any childcare). So I was very much on holiday.

Up in Fife in the snow, I found myself at a meeting about housing. It seemed there was a room or so going in a house in Edinburgh later in the year. I could have it – small girl no problem. The women I'd be sharing with weren't even at this 'meeting'. On my way back down south I did, briefly, meet Cathrine, one of the women I'd be sharing with.

Both then and now I find this amazingly generous and supportive. Quite recently I was reminiscing with a friend about that time and she said 'wimminspace! that was so awful!' – the idea that if wimmin had the use of a house it should be for all wimmin, that any wommin who was homeless had a right to any space that was going in wimmin's houses. And certainly it could make life pretty difficult – however, for me, it got me out of what felt like an awful situation and was what I needed.

Several months of mental knots followed. Those months also included a visit from K, and a bit of violence from the man I was living with. By the time I was able to move out I had started to realise there was going to be resistance. A friend was to drive me, my daughter and our stuff up in a van. She had to come round during the day while the chap was out at work. But he came back and it was a nightmarish day. He tried to lock me in. When that didn't work, there were what seemed like hours of my friends moving my things out of one door, and the chap bringing them back in through the other. He also tried to kidnap my daughter from her nursery school but I'd thought to warn them.

So when I did get up here (after a month spent moving around the country before the room was ours) I was very glad to be a long way away from him and not to have found somewhere handy round the corner! And though the move was supposedly on the way to Fife, I've stayed in Edinburgh ever since, and I'm now extremely attached to the place.

And when I got up here, I'd moved into a supportive community of women – lesbian feminists. In running away from the chap I'd left a lot of my previous existence. In particular, I was starting from scratch without knowing any men. So it was easy not to put energy into men – one way of defining separatism.

You could fill this book with separatists and we'd all have different views and experiences. I chose for women. I've never felt I want to be a lesbian separatist, to spend all my time or energy on lesbians only. It was always 'women only'.

Actually, I never called myself a separatist, though I defended the label. This comes from a kind of purism, of pedantry about precision of meaning. The first member of my family I managed to tell I was a lesbian was my brother, and he was very supportive – in fact he reacted as if having a lesbian sister was the best thing since sliced bread. He still is very supportive, and even when I was most anti-men he has always been my 'exception'.

Separatism involves contradictions. It's about control, but it's also a personal solution coming out of politics that says there are no personal solutions (i.e. that women's position will only change as a result of overall political 'solution'). For all women, any relationship with a man (sexual or not – family or not) is always an exception.

We've all been taught not to trust strange men. We differ over which men we categorise as strange.

Separatism for me was about excluding men from my life as far as possible. There were always men I regarded as exceptions, but I still refuse to see, for example, a woman's lifestyle as separatist if she looks after boys – of whatever age – because, as a mother, I know just how much energy that takes. I can't see that as being on the same level as having my father to stay because I want to spend time with my mother. Those two situations could be seen as degrees of separatism, but I prefer to see the first as non-separatism and the second as separatism with occasional exceptions. For years I've been thinking I don't really believe in this stuff any more, and then as soon as I start talking or thinking seriously about it, it seems that all that has changed is my pragmatic response to the situations I find myself dealing with. Living with a heterosexual teenage daughter cannot be a separatist lifestyle. In saying this I suppose I am admitting that my current lifestyle is different in degree rather than kind from that I might have if I'd given birth to a boy and chosen to look after him.

My daughter was three when I moved up here, and until the end of her first year at school, I didn't know any men here. In other ways my lifestyle hadn't changed much – I was looking after a small child, I was on the dole, I spent a lot of time going on demonstrations, to conferences, visiting friends and having heavyweight discussions!

What was it about the politics that kept me going? It was a kind of clarity about blaming the people in power – basically saying that women's oppression is men's fault. Sloganised – 'it's all men's fault' – this means 'it's all the fault of men', but there was a tendency to feel this as 'it's the fault of all men'. I still find it quite difficult to talk about this in mixed space. I see a lot of holes in it now, but really it does have a kind of radical clarity, and it certainly does make a lot more sense than saying that women are oppressed because of the class system, or because of the system of government. Women are oppressed because men have power. But there's far more problems with simply blaming individual men than I wanted to admit at that time.

The parallel with nationalism started striking me as soon as I came up here. It hadn't really struck me in Wales. When I first lived there, I hung around a lot with Welsh nationalists, and they were very happy to have English supporters, especially ones prepared to learn the language. Basically there was the feeling that anyone who supported the cause was acceptable – which I didn't find among nationalists I met in Scotland. There are a lot of parallels between feeling that I as an English person am being personally blamed for the evils going on in Scotland and saying that even supportive men are personally to blame for the evils of male supremacy.

The Women's Liberation Movement in Britain at that time was much more organised than it is now. It had a national newsletter, *WIRES*, and it had national conferences – the last was in 1978 – as well as special-interest conferences. There was this radical and revolutionary feminist conference in Brighton that I went to in 1978 – the previous one had been in Edinburgh. There were Scottish Women's Liberation Conferences. A lot of the politics was around fighting back against male violence, and supporting women who'd fought back. One big campaign was in defence of an Edinburgh woman who had been jailed for killing her violent husband.

I was also involved in the organising to get the 'new' Women's Centre in Edinburgh, which we still have; and with producing *Nessie*, 'a radical/revolutionary feminist newsletter from Scotland', which, like *WIRES*, was for women only.

When I nostalge about the 'separatist days' it isn't really for the political activity, because it wasn't so different from the political activities I've taken part in (on and off!) either before or since. It's for pictures like my daughter, aged three, shouting in the Meadows 'Maggie and Cathrine hates men in Edinburgh!', or, slightly later, shushing me in a bus for mentioning the women's centre. It's for playing in a women's band that only performed at women-only events. It's for the feeling that everyone in the WLM knew everyone else.

We were questioning everything, absolutely everything. We felt we could change the world! When I re-read newsletters from the late seventies and early eighties, they still seem so radical. So much of what we campaigned for then still seems so far from being realised. Even the Seven Demands of the Women's Liberation Movement* seem pretty radical these days.

Although I'm feeling very distant from separatism at the moment, I want to say how freeing and positive I've found, and can still find, women-only spaces, from social events to newsletters! I love the energy that comes from feeling that special safety. Feeling that it is womenspace rather than 'lesbian' space goes with my belief that every woman can be a lesbian.

I got a high-rise flat in a peripheral estate in 1981, my daughter's second year at primary school. Almost immediately I felt isolated – I felt, in fact, like a single parent, which I never had before, though technically I'd been one all along. Not only was I now living alone with my daughter, I had lost a lot of support with childcare. When I first came to Edinburgh, the women who I moved up to be close to did what now feels an amazing quantity of childcare for me – I really should have said more about that, because it enabled me to do a lot of the other things. All those women moved away from Edinburgh around that time, and only Cathrine has come back again.

Other reasons for my increasing isolation I find difficult to disentangle: I moved, but at the same time all these structures in the Women's Liberation Movement started to disappear. *WIRES* collapsed, conferences dwindled to a halt, and so did a lot of the more political feminist groups in Edinburgh.

Thatcher being in power had a lot to do with it. It's hard to hold on to the idea that it's all men's fault when a woman is so apparently the one responsible for making women's lives harder. I think, also, that Greenham was a really wrong direction for the women's movement. Whatever I or anyone may think about identity politics, it makes sense for women to organise without men against women's oppression. Nuclear weapons, peace – they're not women's issues. They affect everyone.

When we first moved to the estate it didn't seem too bad – it wasn't a 'nice' council estate, but it certainly wasn't a 'nasty' one either. But over the five years we lived there it was becoming more and more teenage gang territory. Quite apart from that, my daughter was got at constantly, almost from the word go, firstly for being different, and secondly for being friends with a Chinese family. She did get hassled at school, but she was got at more, really, every time she set foot outside the flat. It's hard to tell whether she was got at actually because I was a lesbian. I did get shouted 'dyke' at, once in the next estate, but not immediately around the flat and not by anyone who knew who I was. It's hard to tell whether I 'look like a lesbian'. When I tell people, some express surprise, some don't. I don't know whether it was an issue at my daughter's school. In effect, it probably was an issue around the estate in general – it was a general 'strangeness', but that actually came from being a lesbian and being political, and from not being smart, looking poor.

I went on being closeted when my daughter was at high school. At one point a boy in her class, whose mother I'd been friendly with, decided to tell people that I was a lesbian – that seemed to blow over – it's hard to tell whether that sort of thing gets taken seriously or remembered. It was always clear that her teachers, and headteachers, thought it was problematic being from a single-parent family, and would have thought it even more so to have a lesbian mother. I've always felt my daughter has enough with any problems of her own, and the ones the teachers have produced for her, without having people knowing I'm a lesbian as well.

I find it hard to be at all chronological about my ceasing to be separatist. Initially it had nothing to do with politics, but came from my involvement in playing classical music. I did make efforts at first to only play with women. But eventually the music seemed more important to me and so for several years I was politically 'women-only' while playing music in mixed groups. I guess when I first joined an orchestra here I was pretty crabby! But eventually I did start socialising with male musicians, and now I hope I can say some of them are my friends.

Meanwhile, though again I find this hard to pinpoint (but surely AIDS had something to do with it) I started to be open to the idea that gay men might be my political allies, and it was around the end of 1986 that I first got involved with a mixed gay group – GALAS.

A group connected with the Labour Campaign for Lesbian and Gay Rights set up a big national conference in London in May 1987, to start a campaign for positive legislation for lesbian and gay rights. This was (shortly!) before Clause 28 was invented, and before the 1987 general election, when there was some optimism about the possibility of a Labour government. A booklet had been produced prior to the conference – basically a draft for possible legislation. Some people in Scotland who'd seen this booklet decided it would be good to have discussions around it before going to the conference.

Out of these discussions we set up a group which was called GALAS – Gay and Lesbian Action Scotland. I take some credit for inventing that name, which I still think is a good one.

For most of the people who came to the group – including me, but also including several of the men – this was the first mixed gay group we'd been involved in. A decision was made to alternate consciousness-raising meetings with political discussion meetings. People with legal knowledge went through this draft legislation with us trying to work out how it applied to Scotland. It became clear pretty fast that the people who had put it together had a few vague notions that there might be some legal differences in Scotland but hadn't a clue what! I find it shocking that people with the legal knowledge to write that stuff were that ignorant about Scotland.

I had been in mixed political groups between around 1974 and 1979, and certainly for the latter part of that time I experienced the behaviour of the men in them as pretty sexist. GALAS felt better, but then I think the men were very much on their best behaviour. It was a real eye-opener doing consciousness-raising with the men, because, although I'd known a few gay men prior to that, I'd never considered them as political allies, or had any sort of political discussions with them. In the consciousness-raising, a lot of differences came up, but it was really positive for me. Because of the ways in which I'd first come across feminism, my initial 'consciousness-raising' had not happened in c-r groups, but in this case it was the right way round!

Out of the London conference had also come a national organisation, OLGA (Organisation for Lesbian and Gay Action). Along with some other people in GALAS, I got heavily involved in OLGA at a national organising level. I think OLGA was the most nightmarish political experience I've had. I've really forgotten a lot of the details, but I vividly remember a morning weeping around Calton Hill, thinking that people I knew were going to get taken to court by other people in the organisation. People talk about splits in the Women's Liberation Movement, but the WLM had nothing on OLGA! After I left OLGA, I just felt I couldn't face those kind of politics again.

When Clause 28 appeared, GALAS got completely hijacked by SHAG – which is a name I still heartily hate; sure, it stands for Scottish Homosexual Action Group, but basically I couldn't bear to identify with a group that called itself SHAG! I did take part in actions they organised – as a group they were much more effective than GALAS – in a strange sort of way, because how can I say they were effective when the Clause got passed?

No, it's not fair to say that GALAS got taken over by SHAG. What happened was that some of the most active people in GALAS were also involved in setting up SHAG, as an immediate response to the threat of the Clause, and SHAG was doing all the visible political stuff in Edinburgh. Once the Clause came on the horizon, we all just gave up trying to go for the positive changes and started fighting back. So it's all the Tory government's fault.

Meanwhile I'd gone on being involved in producing the *Edinburgh Women's Liberation Newsletter*, which I've been doing since 1984 – even though I sometimes despair at the content and say 'what has this got to do with women's liberation?' It's still there as a means of communication. That's something I feel really strongly about. The newsletter has appeared almost every month since 1982. It's always had a policy of printing everything women send to it. The origin of this policy came from *WIRES* and other WLM publications of the same period. They eventually added riders – everything sent unless against the WLM demands – or unless sexist, racist etc. If we were sent something that was consciously, deliberately sexist, racist, etc., we wouldn't print it, but I've never wanted us to have that kind of censorship policy. It's very difficult to apply. If we're sent something that's controversial, and this usually has been either around class or around issues of sexuality, most of us think it's a good idea to print it and let women reply. Incidentally I've never seen a publication with a policy of not printing anything that was anti-mother. That always made me angry because I think mothers have an added oppression. I've felt more oppressed in this society as a mother than as a lesbian.

I have also, along with other women, sought out and put into the newsletter information about AIDS ever since we first heard of its existence. I'm not going to try to fit into this story how AIDS has affected me personally but I do want to say that it has a lot to do with how distant I feel from separatism right now.

There is so much I've left out – my relationship of the last ten years!

Women Live, through which I met my lover . . . the Lesbian Mothers' Group . . . so many more women's groups – anti-pornography, relationships with children, songwriting . . . my own writing and women's writing groups . . .

I've left out negative stuff too. Lots of political rows. But at least in the WLM we didn't take each other to court. We knew whose side the state was on.

I don't know where I'm going politically at the moment; personal things feel more pressing right now, and I feel very distant from identity-based politics, especially the kind that emphasise people's origins or unchangeable aspects rather than choices.

About debates about the future of Scotland, I feel fairly despairing, because essentially I think Scotland should be independent, but I find it extremely hard to believe this can be achieved without bloodshed. I wouldn't say that except that I so frequently see articles which imply that it will – that the English government will eventually see reason, once we get the right English government. It's hard to tell whether, in an independent Scotland, things would be better or worse for lesbians and gays, or for women generally.

I don't seriously consider going back to England – there isn't anywhere I feel I'd belong. If I've stuck my roots down anywhere they're here. My lover is Scottish – my life's here.

* The Seven Demands of the Women's Liberation Movement
We assert a woman's right to define her own sexuality and demand:

1   Equal pay for equal work
2   Equal education and job opportunities
3   Free contraception and abortion on demand
4   Free 24-hour childcare
5   Legal and financial independence for women
6   An end to all discrimination against lesbians

7   Freedom for all women from intimidation by the threat or use
    of violence or sexual coercion, regardless of marital status; an
    end to all laws, assumptions and institutions that perpetuate
    male dominance and men's aggression towards women.

MARION GRIERSON

(b. 1954)

My name is Marion Grierson and I was born in Dumfries in 1954. My father was a farmworker on his uncle's farm, just four miles from there and so my early days were spent in a cottage on the farm with my older sister, my mother and father. Until going to school, neither of us really mixed much with other children. From a very early age I remember being an outdoor child and my sister an indoor child. We used to bribe each other to play together. I was never happier than if I had hammer and nails or another favourite for me was going down to the burn that ran through the farm and damming it up.

My father was a very quiet, shy, gentle kind of man, Scottish-

born, and my mother is German-born. I think it's quite a consider-
ation that she left Germany when she was nineteen or twenty years
old and came to Britain very much at the end of the Second World
War. My mother landed up having to fit into an environment that
was very hostile and having to learn a language that she didn't know
at all. In years to come people would say, why did your mother never
speak German to you and your sister? At first we thought it was
strange but then we realised that the last thing anybody in the street
in a small town in Scotland wanted to hear was the language of a
country that they'd just been to war with.

It was a very strange background because my father was very
much dominated by his uncle who owned the farm. He was very
much kept in the farmworkers' ranks and uncle would still call my
father, Boy, even when he was in his fifties. The only person who
could really stand up to my uncle was my mother. My great-uncle
was a bachelor and he absolutely thrived on the atmosphere of my
mother arguing with him; he also thrived on dominating my father.
My father always did what he was told because he was always
threatened with – well, this will all be yours one day, boy, and if
you don't do what I tell you, it'll not be. I think he felt he was
trapped. In some ways the best thing they could ever have done
would have been to leave the whole situation but they never did
through lack of money and lack of somewhere else to go. My mother
has definitely never forgiven that situation. My uncle died in 1977
and my father did inherit the entire farm but, unfortunately, he died
suddenly eighteen months afterwards. He really only had eighteen
months of his own life to call the farm his own and actually be his
own boss. I always had a very strong interest in the farm but I always
said there was no way I would ever work for my great-uncle.

When I was thirteen I landed up having really strong feelings for
two girls at school who were sisters. Our friendship developed over
the space of about a year and that was the first physical contact I
ever with either male or female beyond just kissing. It was kissing

and touching but never actually touching each other's genitals. Also at that time I had my first serious boyfriend who stayed in my life for four years. The twins I was so obsessed about – their affections turned to boys but although I had a boyfriend I was reluctant to give them up. They weren't identical but a lot of people could get them confused; I didn't confuse them at all. They were like two individuals but I landed up having really strong feelings for both of them. For the rest of my secondary school days there were no allegiances with women because of the boyfriend I had. It was with him that I actually lost my virginity eventually and he with me and that would be when I had just turned sixteen. On a beach of all places, the worst place in the world to lose your virginity. We stayed together for a year after that and never ever did it again; we never spoke about it.

There were definitely a few teachers at school that I reckoned were gay. I have distinct memories of, for instance, a female art teacher who was then in her mid to late fifties. I was convinced that she was gay but not living a gay lifestyle. She very much liked the girls and hated the boys and also liked some girls more than others. I later went to art college but I always felt that her interest in me was more than just the fact that I was OK at art. I always remember on probably my last day of school going to say goodbye to her and being mortified about the fact that she took my hand in front of a class and stood and talked to me for quite a while; she wouldn't let go of my hand and I was totally embarrassed by this because I got the impression everyone else was watching.

I was very definitely conscious of homosexuality existing but there weren't what you would call any positive images. I can remember going out of a so-called sex education class in tears. It was exactly when I'd just split up with my boyfriend and I can remember feeling totally mixed up. But one of the reasons that I did leave the class was the fact that I was upset that there was no mention of any other kind of lifestyle. I felt that I was sitting there listening to them trying to explain what a heterosexual lifestyle and sexual relationship would be and I just felt that that wasn't for me.

I decided to go to art college because apart from being quite reasonable at art I thought I was sure to meet like souls at art college. But I couldn't have been more wrong. Aberdeen wasn't a particularly large art school. There was an intake of about seventy new students each year which meant that the whole student body was no more than 300. I went into digs with two fellow art students, both called Carol. Needless to say, I got an instant crush on one of them. These feelings stayed for the best part of four years and probably had a major influence on everything I did. The only gay scene that I was conscious of was a gaysoc – gay society – at Aberdeen University. I felt that it was very much university-orientated and probably also very much men-orientated. Nor did I feel any need to be in touch with them at that time. The Carol that I was interested in and I got a flat together. Over the next few years we moved from one flat to the next, Carol having boyfriends and me not having anybody. Carol and I would spend quite a lot of time together and I told her – perhaps in the second year – how I felt. She was very good but felt that she couldn't reciprocate the feelings at all. I did eventually get a boyfriend but my feelings for him weren't serious though we were sexually involved.

After our third year Carol agreed to go on holiday with me. We took an overland bus to Athens and then went island hopping. It was there on a beach, on a Greek island, that I made my move after all these years of waiting because for some reason I just had the feeling that Carol wouldn't say no and she didn't. For the duration of that holiday everything was wonderful and for the first time in my life I was relating to somebody the way I wanted to. What was awful was, literally on the ferry back over the Channel, Carol told me that was it; there was no way once we were back in Britain that the relationship could continue; she'd felt that it was OK to be the way she was when she was in Greece but that she couldn't come to terms with being that way in Aberdeen and that she didn't feel that that was truly the way she was.

I had to come to terms with the fact that Carol felt the way she did but I still felt as strongly as I did. After about two months Carol and I decided we had to split up. I came out to other friends simply because I felt I was going off my head and I just needed somebody else to talk to. These two friends were also Carol's friends so it was very hard for them because they just hadn't had a clue. They suddenly were having to come to terms with the fact that I was gay and also it was hard for them to know how to relate to each of us. But it was one of those friends who actually offered me a room in her flat. But it was a terrible struggle for me emotionally because I literally could feel I was on the point of having a nervous breakdown.

I phoned the Aberdeen Gaysoc number and spoke to a guy who was very helpful and said that he could put me in touch with some women. This was probably on a Friday and by that Saturday I'd arranged to meet some women. This, I suppose, was my first real coming out. I met this person called Rosemary and my first reaction was horror because I thought, I'm not really like you. She was quite butch and hard. She was a real Aberdonian and real down to earth and it turned out I actually got on quite well with her. That night she took me along to a bar called Bells and then to a disco. I was conveniently paired off with this Australian, quite a bit older than me. In one fell swoop in the space of thirty-six hours I went from coming out to going to a gay bar, to a disco, to a party and landed up in bed with a full 100% lesbian for the first time. I had some guilt pangs but I also knew that was where I belonged. I then had all sorts of strange feelings about the fact that I then had to still function in the social life that I was in. I realised that from then on I was going to have two lives and probably keep those two lives separate.

Through those women that night I landed up becoming part of a group that used to meet at a couple's house on Saturday nights. It was absolutely tiny – consisted of one room with a toilet halfway down the landing and that was it. There was probably a group from about eight to twelve people would come and they would be very much drinking sessions. I learned quite early on just how much these women seemed to drink and not only that, I also realised how much they seemed to flirt once they'd been drinking. Once I left Aberdeen I did lose contact with them all. In fact, the only person from Aberdeen days that I'm still in contact with on any kind of regular basis is Carol; we did eventually regain a really good friendship.

I managed to get through my diploma by the skin of my teeth and came home to the farm for the summer. I always worked at the hay and I always enjoyed being on the farm but I still maintained that I couldn't be there with my uncle on a full-time basis. I think my dad was pleased I came home for the time I did, but in the September of that year, 1976, I flew off to Israel. I worked on a kibbutz there and then spent time in Greece and Italy. My great-uncle died in October of 1977 and in January I finally landed back on the farm and that's when I started to work with my father.

Coming back was a very emotionally mixed up time for me. I can always remember crying buckets, absolutely howling and my mother coming into my room to find out. She couldn't understand why I was so upset in my own home town doing what I had always said I wanted to do. My dilemma at that point was the fact that I just could not work at or believe that there was any way I could have a gay lifestyle in my own home town. For starters, not knowing anybody gay, but just knowing how eternally straight everything around me seemed to be. Once again, I landed up getting caught up in a heterosexual relationship. And in order to get back into the swing of things in Dumfries I became involved in a very traditional local event called the Guid Neighbours Festival. It's something that goes on a lot in the Borders towns in Scotland where you always have Riding of the Marches which mostly takes place on horseback. I took part in the Guid Neighbours Festival that year and through that met quite a lot of people including the woman who was to be my lover for the next seven and a half years. Over that year Pat and I would find that when we were in large mixed companies we always seemed to end up speaking to each other despite the fact that she was with a guy and I was with a guy.

In April 1979 I left Scotland to go off to America and it was while I was in San Diego that my father died suddenly. I wasn't able to get back for the funeral and so when I did get back home I was there totally for my mother when everyone else was starting to disappear. The other person who was still on the scene was this guy who I'd been involved with for about a year. Things started to snowball very quickly because there I was twenty-four years old with my mother, no brothers and my father gone. My boyfriend had also started to help out quite a lot and was really quite keen on the farm. The natural course of events in everyone's thinking was that Brian and I should get married as soon as possible. He tried not to seem as if he was pushing in that direction but he definitely was. So I found myself in the situation where I had to come out to my boyfriend and tell him that I thought the relationship should end because that was not for me. I felt a relief and I then could concentrate more on my feelings and thoughts for Pat.

Meanwhile I had joined the theatre of which Pat was also a member. By the end of January 1980 I landed up coming out to Pat and she landed up coming out to me. That was on the Friday and on the Saturday we landed up telling each other how we felt about each other. I also felt that I had to come out to my mother because I felt she must wonder why I was spending so much time with this woman who had a flat in Dumfries and how I was concentrating all my time with her and not really with the rest of my group of friends. So the morning I was going to tell her I was stuttering and stammering over my words. My mother landed up turning round and actually saying to me, I think you're trying to tell me about you and Pat. That was a relief because at least she was conscious enough to have realised what was going on. I couldn't believe how reasonable she was about the whole thing, but sadly we didn't continue to talk about it as time went on.

Pat and I continued to see each other all of that summer. Meanwhile I was doing up the house where I'd grown up as my mother had moved into the farmhouse. Suddenly there was a chance I was going to move there with Pat and that's what happened in October of 1980. Pat and I then entered into a seven and a half year relationship which had lots of ups and downs but was, in the main, very good. Always the thing that endured was the friendship we'd established in the beginning. I think the fact that we got to know each other so well before we became involved was a great grounding for our relationship.

As the time went on, through the Eighties, Pat and I were still very involved at the theatre. One of the things that happened was that, because it is a small town, people very quickly put two and two together and realised the situation. At one point it seemed like the whole town was against us; what happened was that my ex-boy-friend heard the rumour that Pat and I had formed a relationship and he decided to blacken our names. Not only was he involved in Guid Neighbours, being a past Coronet in Dumfries, but he was also a leading light in the dramatic society and so that meant that he had access to absolutely everybody I knew. Before we knew it nobody would speak to Pat and I. The only person who was still supporting us was my mother. There were a couple of friends who, for various reasons, did support us but they didn't like to be seen to support us in front of everybody else. What eventually happened, which was probably quite typical, was that Pat and I became caught up in our own small world and we decided we could survive without everyone else. Eventually some of these other people started coming back into our lives, but the sad thing was that we never felt the same about them anymore.

Being outed also meant that we became more conscious of other gay people in the theatre – all men. One guy had actually been to school with me and I'd always had my suspicions but because he wasn't involved with anybody I was never very sure. Round about the same time I became involved with Pat, he became involved with another guy who was a member of the group and the four of us became very close. What was happening was that there was a conscious group of gay people that revolved mainly round the theatre. Then at one point around 1984–85 one of us noticed an ad in *Gay Scotland* from someone called Douglas asking if anyone interested in meeting other people in the Dumfries area would contact his number. It turns out it was an actual incomer into Dumfries from Glasgow but quite a few of us decided to respond to this ad. There would be about ten people at the first meeting but it was like Douglas had arranged a social gathering for all the people we already knew and he was the odd one out. But that eventually was resolved and he got to know us. And what stemmed from that meeting was the gay group that now exists in Dumfries. It took quite a lot to do it but eventually some kind of social scene was set up and a phoneline and social events in public places. One of the things that is interesting is that the time Pat and I were together – seven and a half years – we never met any other women through the gay group.

My mother introduced Pat and I to two other women whom she was convinced were gay. They'd been together for seventeen and a half years but just as they were the first gay women that Pat and I had met so we were the first gay women they had met in Dumfries. And to cut a long story short that was to be bad news because eventually that was to be the end of both relationships. At first Pat and I didn't speak to each other. That was possibly the best thing that could happen because I split away from all of them and landed up going my own way.

It was through a friend at the theatre that I heard her daughter, Evelyn, was due to come back to Dumfries. I was seven and a half years older than Evelyn and I had met her over the years and I just had this feeling that she was gay. I also knew that it was very much a mistake to become involved with anyone at a time when I was just coming out of a seven and a half year relationship. I had really no other women to talk to because I'd isolated myself. As fate would have it, one day Evelyn and I met in a shop in Dumfries. I must have by then come to terms with who I was and how I felt because in the middle of the shop I just said to her that I was gay and I asked her if she was. It just made her fall over backwards because I don't think anyone had been that forthright with her. She'd just come back to Dumfries having been in the Army for two and a half years and she had been involved in a gay lifestyle but with all the restrictions that Army life brings.

Evelyn and I met on a Friday and we went out together on the Saturday. She knew that everybody knew that I was gay and had a slight hang-up about being seen anywhere in Dumfries with me. So we went down to the Lake District for the night and things just went from there. Over four years later Evelyn and I are still together and this time I was determined to learn from all the mistakes I made in my first relationship. Number one was not to isolate ourselves. I met two other women who were living locally – newcomers to the Dumfries area and through them a network of other women. Four years later there must be at least thirty women who at some point or other socialize with each other. In the space of a couple of years the men's group has gone from eight or ten to perhaps fifty or sixty. The late Eighties, early Nineties have definitely been the coming out years for Dumfries.

I have quite a dilemma as a gay woman coming into contact with the majority of gay women who, it seems, are vegetarians. It's terrible because I always feel I have to justify what I do for a living to some of my friends. It's a 100% beef farm, mainly Aberdeen Angus and quite a lot of Hereford cows. I am almost a vegetarian but I'll always buy steak because I feel I have to support my own industry.

There are hundreds of farmers who see it as a great social thing to go to the market and I can understand that, because there are lots of farmers who don't have a good social life. But I only go to the market when I need to go. There's always plenty of people to talk to and I have great chats with a lot of the older farmers; there's quite a lot of them who knew my dad and my uncle and they'll always make a point of talking to me and I always make a point of talking to them. I think it's good for them that there are the occasional women who go in there in their own right. It makes them think a wee bit more about what women and men can and cannot do because I think the farming community must be one of the most old-fashioned when it comes to men's and women's places.

KEN COWAN

(b. 1955)

I was born in Glasgow in 1955. I was an only child and we moved from Springburn to East Kilbride when I was one and a half. My mother worked for a while as an usherette at the Princess Cinema in Springburn and then for ten or eleven years in a factory in East Kilbride. It was wonderful for me when she was an usherette because I was about four and I could see *Superman* and get an ice lolly. My father was a general labourer – totally unreliable and always getting the sack. He bought an ice cream van when I was about ten or eleven and he did that until he died. They were never used to money and on Fridays we often had chips for tea because the money had run out.

They were both very stern people. I don't think they would have known happiness. My father was illegitimate and there is a whole family of brothers and sisters, none of whom has the same father. They lived in Garngad which was a pretty rough area. My grandmother was a great character; she drank and went round the pubs. She worked as a prostitute to keep the family together and my father remembered getting clothes and shoes from the parish. My mother's side was Donegal Irish and so she was a Catholic. My father was only nominally Protestant but his mother was Orange and there was a great deal of disruption in the family when they decided to get married. I was brought up as a Catholic much to my father's family's disgust.

I enjoyed being brought up in East Kilbride. There were lots of trees and you could play. The outstanding memory of my childhood was when I was about two and a half. There were workmen laying the roads and one of them asked me to come and sit on his knee. I sat on his knee, having sips of his tea while he blethered away. He was so good-looking and I don't know now if he would be fifteen or sixteen or twenty-five. Thirty odd years I can still feel that feeling. It was entirely innocent and it was lovely.

I was a blether as a child and my mother swears blind that I changed when I was about seven or eight and became more quiet and shy. I don't know why but certainly by the age of ten or eleven I was very attracted to other boys. My first sexual experience was with another boy at primary school. He was my best pal and I thought he was the bee's knees. That carried on until second year in secondary school – I went to a senior secondary in Hamilton. Even at that time I was aware that it was just an exploration for him, a kind of transition but I was very sure that it wasn't that for me. Even though we were both acting like, I suppose, poofs, I became frightened that he would think I was a poof.

I was very frightened of the feelings I had for other boys and I tried, quite successfully, to hide them. My teenage years were quite a misery because of all these feelings that I felt I had to keep to myself. I had been quite good at football when I was a boy but after I was twelve I didn't play again. I was actually scared to go into a dressing room in case the rest would spot that I was a poof. I preferred the company of girls because they didnae threaten me in any shape or fashion.

Apart from the sexual thing my teenage years were great. I started to read and I started to discover about the world. I read all the usual things like the Hardy Boys and the Famous Five but by the time I was thirteen I was reading serious novels like Graham Greene and Evelyn Waugh. I had a schoolmaster who liked books and he would give me books and then we could talk about them. I read everything I could lay my hands on and I could switch off from everything around me – the TV, the fights, the talk. I don't know where I would be if these things hadn't been there to sustain me because what I got from my family would not have sustained me. I actually despised their lack of wonder about the world – if you've no wonder about the world, you've got to be narrow-minded.

I enjoyed my last couple of years in school enormously. I was clever and I was doing amateur dramatics and the school magazine. They were the times I felt most relaxed with people. They were my golden years and I still have comfort dreams about them. I was having sex with females off and on, but it was never the real thing. I was falling in love with boys, secretly and quietly and desperately, because I never thought it could be returned in any shape or fashion.

I left school when I was eighteen and went to Strathclyde University. There were quite a number of people from school went there and I lived at home. In the second year I knew I was going to have to get the head down and do some serious work but I didnae want to do it and so I decided to leave. I went to work for the Inland Revenue in East Kilbride. Being an only child I felt the pull and pressure of my parents, maybe in ways that brothers and sisters don't. I worked there for a couple of years and I had some pals. I was starting to get the confidence to say in a very half-hearted way that I thought I might be gay, but that freaked some of my pals.

I knew I had to meet other people. This was in the days before Switchboard and I saw something in a newspaper about the Scottish Minorities Group (SMG). I phoned one of the contact numbers and I was asked to an 'at home' in the West End. Even though I was commuting to Glasgow I didn't know it well and the West End filled me with awe. The Byres Road had all the associations for me of a bohemian lifestyle. I went to this at home one Friday night and for four hours I shook in the company of eight or nine other men. I was so nervous I couldnae hold a cup of coffee and I fled. But the following week I went back.

A man from Blantyre offered me a lift home to East Kilbride. He told me he was married but gay. I thought that he wasn't going the right way to East Kilbride and then he stopped the car and asked me if I fancied getting in the back with him. I said that I'd never done this before but I think at first he thought I was just saying that. I was actually very angry with him because he took advantage of me. He asked me for my phone number and I gave it to him because I didn't know how not to. I was mortified when he phoned the following week. I refused to speak to him and I never saw him again.

I went to an SMG meeting in Clyde Street and from there somebody took me to *Vintners*, a gay pub just round the corner. It was a real eye-opener – packed with young people. I liked it but I was frightened at the same time. I just wanted to meet somebody and settle down, get married – nothing specific but he had to be about six foot, dark hair, good-looking and all that goes along with that. I met some people that I knew there – some from school, some from the Drama Society. Then I met a guy who was three or four years older than me, quite clever, finishing off a Ph D. He would tell me about gay rights and because I'd been political, even as a kid, I got carried up in his protest. He didnae fit all the requirements but I thought – you'll do – and so I threw myself into an affair with him to get myself away from *Vintners*.

By this time I'd moved to Glasgow, got a flat in Hyndland Road and I'd left my job. A week later I got a job with the National Health Service. Life seemed wonderful. I'd taken a religious fit when I was eighteen and I started going to Mass. There was nothing joyous or happy about it – Homi Miserum. When I got involved with Frank I was meeting other gays and there was a whole lifestyle of sex, drugs and rock'n'roll and so the Catholic phase passed. We were together a couple of years and then he had to go down to London to get a teaching job. I was distraught and I realised I didn't know anybody except his friends.

I got involved with the Scottish Homosexual Rights Group (SHRG) because I thought that's how to meet people without getting involved in the sex thing. But I was going to the *Duke* and having quite a lot of sex, mostly one-night stands. I was enjoying that and I was getting involved politically. I was interested in gay rights because I believed at that time that there was a conspiracy to maintain normality and there were all sorts of projects on the go. There was the opening of the gay centre and the blasphemy trial of *Gay News* in 1977. And although I normally voted Labour I was flirting around the edges of Scottish nationalism. I met a couple called Alan and Alison, who were both members of the Communist Party, and I started hanging around with them and their friends in the Communist Party. So you've got this guy who's gay, ex-Catholic, who joins the Party because they're into gay rights and home rule and who's seriously fucked up in the head around issues of sex and relationships.

I was living with another gay man, Len, thirteen years older than me, sensible, good company, into sex in a big way. We shared for seven years and it was very good for me; it became one of my most enduring friendships. But getting involved with all these extreme things was a way of not getting involved with me and not having to look at my part in things. Nobody ever told me before I joined that the Communist Party was seriously factionalised and the personal animosity that was covered up in terms of what was supposed to be politics was quite unreal. I was in the Govanhill branch and I made the sandwiches at all the meetings – the catering corps of the Party. I met other party members who were gay for regular discussion meetings and I started to have a relationship with one of them.

This guy was seriously into Marxism and sex and particularly sex with me. He lived in West Lothian but he was from down South. He was like a lot of party members in that the personal never quite caught up with the political and the political never quite caught up with the personal. He was heavy duty. He would have his fun time and then the fun time would be over and it would be the serious business of union activity and party work and the two never met. We were together for about two and a half years. The first year was OK and I actually thought I was in love. After that I realised I wisnae in love but more to the point he was in love with me. So we crossed paths, as happens in relationships. He also turned extremely possessive and violent on occasion. He'd be so apologetic but he was not prepared to look at the issues. It was about possessiveness and jealousy but he couldn't admit that because it was part of the ideology that they were bad things that you should just do away with. I had good friends and they warned me to stop seeing him because something nasty would happen. It did come to an end and it was OK.

In 1978/79 I was doing away, still working in the Health Service and still a party member. I had a good flatmate. I went out, had lots of sex, got drunk but I look back and I often think it was me doing these things because they make people happy but I'm not sure how happy they made me. And I was really drinking. Parties, discos, weekends. 1979 was the referendum in Scotland and we were robbed of the prize. That had a catastrophic effect on me. Then Thatcher was elected and I was fed up with the internal bickering in the Party. In 1979 everything seemed to come to a stop.

I'd been involved in SHRG when a gay centre had been started in Glasgow around 1977/78. It was a bit small and it began to shut around the time the gay club opened in Queens Crescent. There was a general feeling then that there wasn't a market for discos and the club proved that there was. It was licensed premises with discos at the weekend and one during the week. It was packed to the gunnels at the weekend. You had to join SHRG to get membership and there were twelve hundred members of the club. I was the membership secretary. It was bloody hard work. The first commercial disco to open in Glasgow was *Bennets* and that was in 1982. It opened five nights a week and the minute it opened the club died. It was a most depressing time in the early 1980s with Thatcher, no home rule and the club shut. I left the Communist Party around this time.

There were some people I worked with in the Health Service who knew I was gay and that was fine. But I was also careful because I have always understood that there will be people who will use it against you for other reasons. There's maybe a contradiction in all this because I was involved in liberation politics but it didn't quite carry into my working life. Coming out is a process, it's about an attitude of mind – how I feel about myself rather than just having as much nookie as possible. If friends won't accept that you're gay, then they're not really friends, they're only seeing one side of your character.

I had told my parents I was gay when I was eighteen and I had made them a promise that I wouldnae act on my feelings. When I got involved with Frank it was two years before we spoke to each other properly. I remember my mother saying that she'd have to move if the neighbours found out. It's transferred shame. She's better now but the truth is that we havnae made up. I always wanted a nice liberal middle class family where they just said – that's OK. There were always conditions put on me by my mother – I love you if . . . I love you but . . . and that is very much the culture of the West of Scotland.

I bought a flat in 1982 and became 'respectable'. Then in 1983 I met a guy who fulfilled all the criteria for Mr Right. I must have been just ready for it. He was dark and chunky, but only five foot six; his name was Billy. I met him one week and he moved in the next. We got married basically. He's five years younger than me, from Easterhouse and was unemployed at the time. It was idyllic for long periods. We had very different interests. He had no politics and he was into personal growth and relationships with people. People buzzed around him; he was very attractive; and I was very flattered that he had chosen me. He got a part-time job and did his self-improvement courses. He was wonderful around the house. We had some good times.

Billy was a very self-controlled, self-motivated individual and he didnae drink. I rather liked that because I felt I had very little motivation, very little self-discipline. And I was really drinking. We split up in August 1988. He had got himself a full-time job and he wanted to buy a flat. I'd felt the relationship with Billy was the last gasp for me and I was very unhappy when we split up. In September my father died of cancer and I was a wreck. I wisnae getting over the fact that Billy had left and I wisnae getting over my father's death. In March 1989 I attempted to stop drinking through counselling at Alcoholics Anonymous and I have not drunk since.

That changed my life entirely. I started to feel that life had some purpose to it. I blamed myself for a lot of things and I blamed Billy for a lot of things and I blamed my family for a lot of things. But things started to pick up and I started to go out. I was enjoying living. From August 1988 I had no sex because I was incapable of having a sexual relationship. I was getting over Billy and I saw him occasionally. The friends I had stood by me and I was sober and I was feeling confident and I was meeting people.

In January 1991 I was diagnosed HIV Positive which was absolutely devastating. I hadn't really thought about it very much over the previous couple of years. I never thought I was going to be

Ken Cowan

touched by AIDS. I'd gone to my GP because I'd been exhausted, had
sore throats and colds that wouldn't go away. She suggested I take
the test. I had a very low T cell count and I was on AZT within four
days. It's been readjustment ever since. It's not the most traumatic
experience – that was stopping drinking. Some of my experiences
at AA helped after the diagnosis because they encourage you to look
at yourself and see how you are rather than try to change the world.
I learned more since I stopped drinking and since I was diagnosed
than in the previous ten years.

I gave up work because it was clear to me that my body was
suffering from me working fifty hours a week. I've never regretted
that. I would be unhappy sitting at home playing around in my head
with what AIDS does. So I got involved in Body Positive and I go
and talk to groups about safer sex. I am a full-time AIDS activist. I'm
making an impact on them because I'm the first person they've met
whom they've known to have HIV. As somebody who got involved
with SHRG in the Seventies I feel that there are whole areas of civil
rights that need to be improved. I am sceptical of most AIDS
professionals because there's a great deal of talk but not a lot of
understanding or commitment. Service provision in Glasgow is not
very good and, in terms of survival, there are issues about moving
to Edinburgh where better facilities are available.

Telling someone you've got the virus is a difficult area. If you're
into a relationship do you tell them on the first night or the first
week or when they've moved in? People work out how to do that as
best they can. If I was involved with somebody and they didn't know
I was HIV I would not only be dishonest towards him but also to
myself. We had assumptions during the Eighties that HIV was only
occurring in San Francisco or London but the virus has been around
doing its work in Glasgow for years. I must have been infected for
years without realising it. This is going to be the real issue for gays
– what are you doing around this area? are you practising safer sex?
I know a lot of gays are adjusting well now and are practising safer

sex. There never really has been a gay community but these issues around survival and death are going to make a gay community.

COLIN MORRISON

(b. 1960)

I was born on May 31st 1960 in Edinburgh. The same
month I was born my family moved into a new house in Muirhouse,
one of Edinburgh's peripheral housing schemes. It seemed like the
middle of nowhere; the buses didn't go that far and there were no
shops. I can still remember smelling the farms. My dad was origi-
nally a gas fitter and then he moved into the training side and now
he's a lecturer in the building trade in an FE college. My mum went
back to work when I was five as a kitchen assistant in the primary
school that I went to just opposite the house. I have one older sister.
My dad's from a family of nine and my mum from a family of thirteen
and so there were lots of family things at the weekends when I was

a kid. I remember doing a family tree at school and sellotaping all the bits together. I had sixty-odd cousins and mine was bigger than anybody else's. Even then there was a lot of poverty in Muirhouse but we were comfortable and had holidays every summer by the sea. My memories of being a child are happy ones.

I was always fairly sociable and outgoing, even in primary school. I was also top of the class in primary one and teachers said to my mum and dad that I would do well. I mixed with most people, girls as well as boys. When the boys were away playing football and boys only stuff, that didn't interest me. My dad was a footballer and a referee and I suppose it was good that I was never pushed in that way. I don't know how they justified it to themselves but I was allowed to do what I wanted to do. As I got a bit older, it became a more conscious, rebellious sort of thing but even in primary school and at the beginning of secondary school I wasn't interested in the football and the girlfriends and all the trappings. I'm absolutely sure that I knew I was gay when I was about ten. I didn't have a word for it but even at that pre-pubescent stage I knew who I wanted to have relationships with; it was about wanting to be closer to males physically than females.

We moved from Muirhouse when I was eleven. The housing policy then seemed to be to abandon families with particular needs in areas like Muirhouse without any support. There were eight families on our stair and two prostitutes working from there. One was fine, a good neighbour, but there was a lot of aggravation about the other one. The whole area was getting pretty heavy and there was a lot of violence and it was difficult to bring kids up there. We were able to get re-housed in Abbeyhill and from then on I spent my life living in the centre of town.

By the time I was thirteen or fourteen, I knew people had relationships with people of the same sex and I didn't have any doubts in my mind that that was something I wanted to do. I think the last time I pretended to have a girlfriend was when I was thirteen but it didn't get very far because I just wasn't interested. I never spoke to anybody about it. I've since met a couple of people from the same school who'd been involved in relationships with people the same age but nothing like that ever happened to me, unfortunately. I remember feeling I was just biding my time until I could be adult enough to go to college. There was a lot of respect in my family for me having some space and so if my friends were round they would be in my room and my parents were never into checking up on who I was with or where I was going. My parents were Labour voters and they always had good traditional values about having respect for people. So it was always made clear to me that people shouldn't suffer some kind of discrimination because they were black and my mother was very strong about women being able to do what they want to do. All that transferred to things about sexuality quite easily.

I remember in my mid-teens discovering that Marc Bolan and David Bowie and Bryan Ferry and people like that had lyrics to a lot of their songs that conveyed images that were very strongly sexual and homosexual as well. It was like they represented a lot of the things I felt. I didn't have access to any books or magazines but I remember going to a cinema in Randolph Crescent in the West End to see a film by Fassbinder – *Fox*. At the time I really enjoyed the openness of the images. That was 1975, about the same time as *The Naked Civil Servant* was on TV. It was safe to talk about these with some friends at school but I probably wouldn't have felt so safe talking about them with the people I was attracted to.

When it came to applying to college, I tried to go away from Edinburgh. I was offered a place at Manchester University but was told that I would have to do another year at school. I didn't want to do that and so staying in Edinburgh was the only option. But that was no problem; Edinburgh's a comfortable place to be and I've always liked staying here. So at the age of seventeen I went to Moray House to do a BEd course. It was a relaxed place, easy to meet people, and it had a history of gay men being about. It was also quite a radical place for student politics. I didn't work particularly hard and I just got by academically because I was heavily involved in the Students Association and the Gaysoc. The year after, the Anti-Nazi League were big and there was a Gays Against the Nazis group. We had a big festival in Craigmillar and a demonstration of about five thousand people. I really enjoyed all that and it was through this political activity that I met Susan whom I still share a house with.

I met somebody at Moray House too and started having a relationship with him within three or four weeks of being a student. He was in the final year of the BEd course and after two or three weeks of going for a drink, going to the cinema, I spent a night with him and that relationship lasted a couple of years. I was, in one way, picked up, but I knew what was going on and I was probably more in control than he thought. It was pretty much one to one but not all the time. It was a good relationship. He was ten years older than me and so I had access to more interesting people and he had a flat and a nice lifestyle. I was younger but I wasn't manipulated in any way and I felt I had an equal part to play. I was given a lot of space to learn new things. I was not very subtle in the way that I ended the relationship when I met someone else. I did hurt him and it was only in the last few years that we've spoken about it. It may seem a bit stupid and a bit patronising but I'm really grateful to him that I had that experience really early on. I've known other people not feel very comfortable in their first experiences but I was lucky to get what I wanted.

I would never say that I was a punk but in the late Seventies I wore mostly second-hand clothes, earrings and a lot of make-up – quite camp basically. I looked quite outrageous to some people, particularly when my hair was dyed. People make a lot of assumptions about appearances and, when I had bleached blonde hair, that seemed to lead people to think I was stupid or less able. When I was a student governor, I was known to be gay, my hair was dyed, I had a working class accent and I didn't have the butchest or deepest of voices. I think I managed to use that to my advantage rather than let people take a loan of me and I don't think it disadvantaged me.

I was still living at home, technically, between the ages of seventeen and nineteen. My mother found this letter and that's how they found out I was gay, but how they hadn't guessed is beyond me. There was a big argument and I stormed out of the house to return two or three months later. It wasn't really talked about after that unless it was about my hair or my clothes or whatever. I was still their son – they had that kind of attitude. But my dad, in particular, would be quite outraged and angry because he thought that was me advertising my sexuality. If it became too noticeable, then that was too much for them. Later on, they became much more positive about sexuality and if they saw something on the telly or in the papers they would raise it and if it were negative say that that was terrible. It was like they'd saved things up until they had something positive to say but it was part of their way of handling it never to say things about me.

I moved in with friends not long after I returned to my parents' and Susan and I still share a house now. When I was finishing my course in 1981, most of us in the house were unemployed. We were very poor and things were basic but our life centred around a good social life as well. Benefits weren't as bad as they are now and when a giro arrived you would go out and have a good time. I preferred then, and still do now, to go to mixed places where being gay isn't a big issue. I had gone to gay places like the *Kenilworth* but they were usually predominantly male. I thought *Fire Island* was always pretty crap. I preferred the kind of parties that there were around the Art College. I'd much rather be in a mixed club where people can go and be comfortable. The music was mostly dance-oriented stuff and there's always been a lot of gay people around as DJs or running them. There was *Dancetria*, around 1980/81. The name was copied from a New York club and that was in *Valentino's* near Tollcross. There was the *Hoochie Coochie Club* too. The people that would go to these clubs would be gay, art college students, punks, fairly mixed. We'd be going out two or three nights a week – the club scene since has changed because of the amount of violence around.

I began to get involved in youth work after being on the dole for a while. It was through the Community Programme that I began working at a new adventure playground in Pilton. It was supposedly an adventure playground with people from five to twenty-five and their Dobermanns and their hassles as well. I enjoyed it but it was really tiring and the wages were shitty and there was not a lot of support. But it was a foot in the door and it led to me doing a Community Ed. postgraduate sandwich course at Moray House. I've always been out with the people I've worked with and with the young people when it has been relevant. There's no point in declaring that you're gay immediately because it can cause a lot of hassle. If asked, I would never lie but if I'm not sure how it's going to be taken or used then I would say that it was a very difficult question and I would ask why they wanted to know. But where the relationships have been good and I've said 'yes' we've been able to talk about it and it's never ever caused me a problem. I've met people in pubs or bars who came to the adventure playground where I worked ten year ago and it's nice to see them out now.

I continued to be involved politically in the Eighties. Some of us set up a Lesbian and Gay Support the Miners Group during the miners' strike of 1984/85. We decided not to give money directly to the NUM and twinned up instead with the Miners' Welfare in White Craigs in East Lothian. All through the winter we used to collect outside the *Laughing Duck* on a Friday and Saturday night. We weren't allowed in. We got called poofs by people on the way past and various other things by people on the way in. It was a strange experience going to White Craigs. We would be going out every week with money to the Miners' Welfare and we would be giving Christmas cards to all the kids with a tenner inside. The mums were opening the cards with the kids saying – oh, this is from the Lesbians and Gays Support the Miners Group. Upfront in one way but at the same time there wasn't any real discussion about it and when the strike was over, that was it. The practicality of it was that we gave a fair bit of money to people who needed it and made a point about lesbian and gay politics in the politics of supporting the miners.

A couple of years after that a group of us heard that the café in the Gay Centre in Broughton Street would be for lease. There were six of us – four men and two women – and we set up a co-op and got furniture, a coffee machine and stuff from the breweries and so on. There had been a tacky café there but we wanted to set up somewhere more like *First Out* in London. We ran it for about a year and a half and it changed character a lot from what it had been before. More women started to use it and that improved the atmosphere a lot; also people who worked locally like social workers and so on began to come in. It was all very stressful and there were problems with the bank and the licensing authority. If we'd been able to expand it would have worked but it wasn't going to and so we decided to get out and it was taken over by the people who have it now. The place is really comfortable now and it looks better than it did when we had it. I'm really glad it's there but I think people often don't realise how things appear. Apart from the bookshop, the café is one of the few things in Edinburgh that has lasted.

I began to feel that I would like to do something as an individual about AIDS. I knew more and more people who were positive but I didn't want to get involved in the politics of SAM (Scottish AIDS Monitor). AIDS has had such a profound effect on everything. Before AIDS being gay was about being really strong and if you wanted to outrage people then you did it. It's a really difficult thing to come to terms with; we've got to change our lifestyles. I've never lived a lifestyle that's been about having sex with people that I didn't know but it's still affecting me. I don't think it's a gay issue but the reality is that it affects us, it affects drug users, and it affects prostitutes and we've all got to face up to it. If other people ignore it, it will eventually be their day as well and they'll have to face up to it; I don't think many heterosexual men have done that yet. I've seen people really ill and that scared the shit out of me. There are young people who I worked with on my first job in Pilton who are dead now or quite ill. I think for me as well it's a big issue politically because it's about class and about poverty. It's going to be more of a problem for poorer families in West Granton than it is for families who can afford care and education – just like it is in Africa.

I got involved with SAM as a buddy and that was really difficult because the people were mostly gay men attempting to work with drug users or ex-drug users. A lot of the buddy stuff has been copied from America but the folk we were working with in Edinburgh didn't want us to go to the doctors or walk their dog or cook them a meal. It was real crisis stuff. I attempted to do that with two people, one of whom I'd known before and liked a lot, but I didn't feel that comfortable with it and decided I didn't want to continue with it. It made me face up to quite a lot of things and it does concern me that people aren't that prepared for how AIDS is going to affect us.

Around 1989 some of us began to talk about setting up a support group for lesbian and gay teenagers. I'd once applied for a job like that in London but there was nothing much around in Edinburgh in terms of support for young people. I'd had concerns about age limits and safeguards and so we thought it would be good to develop something that was managed by people who were already experienced in working with young people. That's how the Stonewall Youth Project was set up for teenagers in Lothian. It's had ups and downs but I feel it's something useful and could be much bigger and better if it was funded and developed properly. It gets some funding from Lothian Region but it needs to have a much more upfront image as well as its own premises. As things are, it's more likely to be young people with access to a private phone, access to a bit of money to get to the group who take part; it's difficult for young women who're looking after their younger brothers or sisters. I'd like to see it much more available to working-class teenagers on the peripheral housing schemes where I think it's had very little impact.

Ever since I left home I've always lived with a group. The first flat there was three of us and then four and the last ten years it's been basically the same group – and it's been added to every now and then by a partner moving in. I was going out with Angus for two and a half years and living together for about a year and a half. When that split up, we decided we still had to work at it and we still live in the same house; it's maybe been a better friendship than relationship; it's worked out. It's always been living together, eating together, sharing things when there wasn't much money around. Even now, we still try, if we can get it organised to eat together. And financially we are dependent on each other to keep the house going. My partner, Kenny, and I have been together for eight years, three of those living together here. I think we're good together, it works out well. There's a baby, Molly, and that's nice – it seems like there's a future.

ANN

(b. 1961)

I was born in Aberdeen in 1961 and grew up in Buckie. My father's a fisherman and has a fishing boat. My mother was a housewife and she works in a papershop that she owns half of. I think the church played a big part in my parents' outlook. They believed that you should work hard and you would reap the benefits. They thought that people who were unemployed were scroungers. They were Baptists – really the Church of Scotland, but different. I went to Sunday school until I was around fifteen and I decided that I didn't care how much I hurt them I wasn't going to go anymore. When I was about six I had a really big crush on my babysitter but when I was eight she and her family moved to London. I was broken-hearted and thought I would never feel that way about anybody again.

We didnae have sex education at all at school. Oh aye, we had a film at primary school about how to have babies. It was for primary five upwards and the headmaster and all the teachers were there – that was really a joke for everybody. In secondary school it was the job of the typing teacher to teach sex education and she let us do our homework. So that was sex education. There was the usual jokes in the playground. They called them lezzies and the boys poofs if they wanted to get at anybody. It was a homophobic atmosphere I was growing up in even though it wisnae mentioned and nobody suspected anybody. In secondary school there were girls that I was close to but I never wanted it to go further and I just felt that they should be my pal. I played a lot of sport with boys and they asked me out to discos. I didnae go and I always made out that it was my mother who wouldnae allow me to go but if I had pushed it with her I would have been allowed. I stayed in a lot and played records on the hi-fi in my room.

In my last two years at school I got close to a teacher through hill walking. We were away on a residential and there was this Abba record playing – 'When I Kissed The Teacher'. She said that she knew who I was thinking about when I heard that song and that really panicked me a lot. I couldnae handle it but she made it plain that if anyone wanted to go hillwalking they should contact her. That led to me going to her flat and she kissed me. I thought that this was what I'd been waiting for and took the opportunity for a few kisses. She said that she'd guessed I knew about her but I didnae. There was one time when my mother said she was going to Inverness and I invited the teacher round to my house. There was nothing happening but my mother came back and thought the worst. After that the teacher felt she had to leave the close-knit community because she couldnae afford to have this come out and I think my mother put a wee bit of pressure on her. I felt that she kind of left me stranded when she moved to Aberdeen and we did not keep in touch. But I was never confused; I knew it was good for me that all the frustration I'd felt between fourteen and sixteen had suddenly gone. I didnae question my sexuality; I knew that's how I would lead the rest of my life. That's when I decided I had to get out of Buckie.

Buckie's got about six thousand people. It's a fishing town and there's farming and ship building and there was the bulb factory but that's closed. The men go to sea and they're seen to be the real providers and if women go out to work, unless they own their own shops, they're looked down upon. When girls left school they had two options: they could go to the fish houses or the bulb factory and if they were really lucky they might have got a job in the office. It was a very enclosed community and people didnae move unless they had a specific reason. Even people who go to university come back and teach or pick up some other job in Buckie. At the youth club the girls would just stand around and watch while the boys played football or pool and the youth workers were mums and didnae discuss issues or any other stuff. I stopped going because I wasn't getting anything out of it. I didnae have any loyalties to Buckie and I knew that staying there would just frustrate me. I decided I'd join the Air Force. My mum wisnae too happy about it but she'd had a friend who'd been in the Navy and had raved on about it. I got away with it because of her but it's funny that I never thought that she might be a lesbian even though she's never married.

I joined the Air Force and I was whisked down to England to do my training in Lincolnshire. I started to meet new people, people with different attitudes and that's really when I started to live. I was a wee bit disappointed when I realised that I should have joined the Army because that's where all the dykes were. But I thought that something would come of it. I didnae know about *Gay Times* or gay switchboards and so I used to scan the personal ads in the newspapers to see if a woman was advertising for another woman. I'd done that with the *Press and Journal* when I lived in Buckie and so I did that in Lincolnshire too. It didnae take me long to find a woman, to bump into somebody but she wasn't a lesbian. She was straight and she was living with a guy. I did half my training at Heathrow and she was working there as a civilian.

One night, because of my trade, I had to go to a party that her dad was giving. He was a diplomat and I didnae want to be at the party because it was too high falutin for me. I was told what to wear and I was very conscious of my Scottish accent in a southern atmosphere. We were both surprised to see each other but to me she was a friendly face. For the previous week I'd noticed that she'd been really quite bruised around the face and that night she was upset. When I asked her about it she explained that the guy she was living with was going through a bad patch and he was taking it out on her. She was sick of it and wanted him to move out of her flat. Because she was quite scared of him I invited her up to Lincoln for the weekend. It was nice and I never thought anything about having a relationship but she was good to me and she was relieved to come up to Lincoln and get away from him. When I finished my training at Heathrow we were both sad and I suggested she could put in for a transfer to Humberside. She said that she might; she came from Norfolk and liked the country and didn't really like London that much. Nothing more was discussed and then one weekend she told me that she was falling in love with me and needed to spend a lot more time with me. I was pleased and things happened and the relationship started and went on for almost four years.

She got a transfer up to Humberside and moved in with me. I was eighteen and she was twenty-two and we were both really inexperienced about same-sex relationships but we just ploughed into it. The Air Force was really homophobic and the rules and regulations say you canny be homosexual. It was a privilege for me to be living off the station and the only way I could do it was to buy my flat. If they'd thought I was moving in with a woman they would have chucked me out. You just had to be hush hush and I couldnae speak about my private life when I was on camp. I was always terrified to be found out and so I couldnae be myself there.

About three weeks after she moved in with me she went all moody and I thought she didn't like me anymore. One day she just started to cry and told me she was pregnant. I thought that she would go back to him but she was adamant that she wasn't even going to tell him. I was a bit confused about that but she was the one who was pregnant and I really left the decisions up to her. We were inseparable and went everywhere together and I just accepted the fact that she was going to have a baby. She was the one who started to have doubts. We wanted to sort things out and went away on holiday to Greece. She shouldnae actually have flown; she was like a beached whale. She was scared about the future and I had to reassure her that I loved her and I was sure I would love the baby. She didnae want the father to know and under no circumstances was she going to tell him. She didnae see it as being unfair. She decided she would go back to work once she had the baby and we would get a child-minder. I didn't actually see Sarah being born and I regret that now but I was there about an hour after she was born. When I seen her the first time, it hit me – God, here's a wee baby and what do you do? I was there along with all the other dads and babies and Jan had an English accent and I had a Scottish accent and they wondered what I was doing there. Then they came home and Sarah and Jan and I continued as a wee family.

I spent a lot of time with Sarah and watching a baby grow up was good. I still had to be very careful about what I said to people at work because of the RAF's rules and regulations. We'd established friends outside the Air Force – straight couples and single people – and they must have suspected about us but we were accepted by them. Jan had come out to her parents and her father was OK but her mother was furious. She never accepted the wee lassie and Jan didnae want anything to do with her if she couldnae accept Sarah. My family found it strange that I was sharing my house with another woman and her baby and though they never mentioned it I think they knew what our relationship was. When we went up to Buckie we used to share the same bed and Sarah used to get a wee crib in our bedroom.

Then Jan died in a car crash. She'd just taken Sarah to the childminders and I was on night shift and she was coming to pick me up. I was coming off shift and the shift coming on were talking and I knew, instinctively, that something was wrong. I always remember one comment – it must be her because it's her car. I opened the door and this woman just went – Right – and I knew. I just left. My boss was through in his office and I just walked out. I walked out of the camp and I saw all this . . . there wisnae an ambulance, it was a police car there. We had a wee sports car and what had happened was that she'd gone under a lorry. It didn't really hit me until about a year after because of the speed things happened but I was stunned.

It wisnae just the case that Jan died but there was Sarah as well. I went and picked Sarah up from the childminders and Jan's parents were sent for. I thought that this would bond them but Jan's mother made it perfectly clear that she wisnae going to bring Sarah up. Social work had to be called and arrangements to have Sarah adopted were made within about three days. That's when I started to get angry about homosexuality and realised that you didnae have any rights at all. Up until then, it was really just plain sailing for me. But I had brought Sarah up and played a big part in bringing her up and we had developed a close relationship and I remember this social worker just picking her up and taking her out the house and I was told very little. I was told eventually that she was going to foster parents and then she would be adopted and, like, nobody asked me. I suppose I could have made a bigger impact but because of the fear of me being found out and thrown out of the RAF I just shut up. I don't know where Sarah is now. I had no contact with her after that.

My boss told me to disappear for a fortnight and when I went back, the Falklands War was in full swing. That was the end of May 1982 and I had to go over there with him. I was still in shock and it seemed that nobody cared. But nobody knew. They just thought this was a friend of mine and it was tragic but maybe the best thing to do was to get out of it. In the Falklands I had plenty time, plenty space to think about just exactly what happened and that's when I decided I would leave the Air Force. Just when the war was finishing I took some time out myself and disappeared. I'd been forced into the war and I had to deal with lots of men crying because they were getting letters saying their wives had left them and I had to deal with other people's stuff. Maybe in a way that was good because I could easily have cracked up. So I disappeared and nobody knew where I was for nine weeks. I went to remote places where there were farms and made quite good friends that way. I didnae sleep rough; I slept in people's houses. My whole life was turned upside down because of the war and Jan and I just had to get my head together because I knew I was coming back.

When I came back I got angrier and angrier with the Air Force about how much control they had over my life and the fact that I had gone through a really traumatic period and I couldnae even share that. I still wanted to come out of the Air Force and then I was posted to Aberdeen. I started to get my life together and, for the first time in my life, I phoned Lesbian Line. I went to a few meetings and they just used to sit and have coffee and chat about women's issues. I had had a good relationship wi' Jan and I was fairly experienced in a lesbian relationship but I hadnae actually come out and I didnae know very much. I remember this woman saying to me – Have you been out in Aberdeen before? And I thought – of course, I've been out in Aberdeen before, I go shopping there every week. She was trying to ask me if I'd been out on the scene. That just showed me how inexperienced I was to the lesbian way of life. I'd never been out because Jan and I hadnae gone to gay bars and we didnae know any other gay people. I didnae know that gay bars existed until I sat down and thought, of course, they've got to exist. I dealt with all the other stuff that was going on in my life and then I thought that I wanted to meet another woman. So I went to Aberdeen on a Friday night week after week and depending on the shifts I was on, I would go to the disco. It was called *Daisy's*. It was a right dive but it was my first taste of the gay scene.

I was very nervous of going to *Daisy's* because it was often raided by the Police and I didnae want to be thrown out of the Air Force. I wanted to leave on my own terms. I started to meet a few of the women in Aberdeen and they were either at university or were social workers or community workers. I began to get interested in their lives and the freedom that they had and it brought home to me just how trapped I was. With one thing and another it took me twenty-eight months to leave and at one point I had to go back to the Falklands for four months. I'd started to see this woman and she was a social worker and so I got interested in social work. When I came back from the Falklands this woman and I started to live together and that relationship lasted for seven years. I came out of the Air Force and that was a big relief. There was still a lot of stuff I had to go through and for six months I didnae do anything. I sold my car and bought this old Mini for fifty quid and for the first time in my life I didnae have to keep up appearances. I loved that Mini. We had a big farmhouse in the middle of nowhere and that was good because it provided things for me to do like chop wood. I quite enjoyed painting and decorating and taking things to bits. The woman I was having the relationship with got a job in Edinburgh and we moved into suburbia and I liked that as well.

We bought that house and we didnae go into contracts and what we would do if we split up because we were quite solid and we didnae think we would split up. We didnae really socialize that much. We sometimes used to go into *Key West* on a Tuesday. We had friends from Edinburgh and friends from Aberdeen and we went hillwalking every weekend. I learned a lot from her about social work, about socialism, about the lesbian and feminist movement. I really had her up on a pedestal. It ended quite abruptly and there was a lot of aggro about other women and about the house. We once had a fight. I was determined not to move out of the house and we had to go to solicitors. We were having surveys done and that was adding to the legal costs. So that was sad how that relationship ended.

When I came down to Edinburgh I had to look for another career. I did a lot of voluntary work and I had a paid youth worker's post. The job was in a wee, very old fashioned homophobic mining village in West Lothian. It wasnae the kind of youth work I wanted to do but it was a taster. I was also doing adult education and work with older people and support work with prostitutes. And I did support work with a single parents group and a lot of that was with very young mums under eighteen. Then I went for this eighteen-hour post at Wester Hailes. I was in at the deep end because I was so green to city kids and I didnae know anything about drugs. That was a good time in my life because I'd begun to feel like I was staid in so many areas and there I was working with the drugs scene and understanding it. While I was there I decided I wanted to do youth work full time or community education. I applied to Moray House and it was late when I applied but I got accepted and I felt so good about that. I got a lot out of the course and it helped a lot when I was splitting up. I was out on the course to lecturers and other students and I was mixing with gay friends and I became quite a strong person.

While I was at Moray House I was involved in setting up the Stonewall Youth Project for lesbian and gay teenagers in Edinburgh. I got a lot from Stonewall. I feel I've had a good working relationship with Colin, the other worker. I'm ready to move on now. I met another woman on one of my placements and I've just started another job in Dundee. Who knows what the future will bring?

ROBIN MITCHELL

(b. 1963)

I was born in 1963 and I lived in Largs until I left home to go to university. I have two older sisters and one younger brother. My mother is a school teacher; my father had a varied career before running the house as a guest house for several years. He went to university at the same time as I did and he was a lecturer in economics and marketing until he died in 1992. We were a close family up to a point and my parents had very little of a social life which didn't involve each other. It is a big house which needs a lot of upkeep and that's how my parents spent much of their free time. My dad would be pottering about in the garage or cleaning the windows. My dad was very political but he very rarely talked about politics with his children. When he died my mum said he probably did believe in God but he'd never suggested within living memory that that was the right way to do things and he had never encouraged us to go to Sunday School. I think a lot of things he didn't really approve of he kept bottled up because he didn't know how to talk about them. I think I'm very much like him in that respect. My mum's not religious. She's very easy-going and takes things in her stride.

I don't remember going out to play very much until I was in Primary Seven and all the boys in my class joined the Boys Brigade and I thought that this is obviously what one does. But it wasn't my cup of tea – it was too sports-orientated – and I was only in the BB for a year. I started playing a brass instrument in Primary Seven and I joined the school orchestra. I was singing in different choirs and I was in the church choir although I was never religious. My circle of friends were all involved in music but I wouldn't say I had close individual friends. I liked to be doing things and not to feel that time was just passing me by.

My parents never talked about sex but my dad once took me aside and told me how babies were made; I had no curiosity about this at all. This must have been pretty late because I'd found out about that in my First Year at school. I was in the art class and this boy who was presumably as naïve as I was said – does your willy get hard when you see pictures of naked women? Before I got the time to say – don't be ridiculous – somebody else piped up, all sort of know-all – of course it does, how else do you think you get it inside a woman to make babies? I was thirteen and that was the first time I'd ever heard of the notion. That was just before I realised I was gay.

I didn't think much about all that until a year later when I was in bed and I got a hard-on. I said to myself – it's not women that give me a hard-on, it's men; so I must be a poof. What I knew about poofs was what I read in the *Daily Express* about gay love affairs and poofy priests. My only image of being gay was your Larry Grayson or John

Inman or your Boy George. There was no one around me that I could identify with. I'd never heard of anyone in Largs being gay. At the very start I thought that maybe I would change and that this was just a phase but after a while I realised that I'd been in this phase for quite a long time. I presumed that everyone else would be horrified if they knew my secret and I was very frightened of being 'found out'. Nonetheless I resigned to it from early on and I decided that my goal in life was to meet other people like me. I had absolutely no idea how to go about this.

When I was fifteen and sixteen I was going round with a mixed group of people who were involved in music and one of them lost his virginity when he was sixteen and we were all aware of it. This made me feel more and more awkward and I felt that my 'difference' was becoming more obvious. So for about nine months I went out with a girl and we would go to parties and family events and she didn't seem at all bothered that I wasn't making any move to take the relationship further. But I felt very guilty about it all and I eventually gave her some lame excuse for calling it off.

I got into a couple of situations at teenage parties where I wished I wasn't there. After I'd finished with my girlfriend I was at one of those parties teenagers have when their parents are away and they get lots of booze and put on records and end up all rolling about the floor together. There was a girl from school who was very keen on me and we ended up snogging on the floor and her hand started wandering towards my zip. I realised I was heading for a really embarrassing moment if I couldn't get a hard-on. I hurriedly excused myself and went and locked myself in the toilet where I tried my best to get a hard-on. It turned out to be an impossible task and so I spent the rest of the night trying to avoid her. She thought I was really weird and I never did that again.

I remember one time when I was about sixteen I was really frustrated and I discovered that there was a football team staying in the hotel next to us for about ten days. These men were presumably in their mid-to late-twenties and lean and fit and when they came back to the hotel after their training they would strip down and parade about between their rooms and bathrooms. My bedroom looked directly over to three of their hotel rooms and after I discovered this I was completely entranced. Some of them were just fab looking and because the bottom of their windows caught them just above the groin I couldn't tell whether they had nothing on or not. This of course drove me up the wall. It was like something from *Rear Window*. When I was supposed to be doing homework or music practice I was in the bathroom or the bedroom next to it trying to work out the way to get the best view without being spotted, experimenting with bits of cardboard on the glass. For about ten days I was completely obsessed.

The other thing that drove me round the bend was this guy at school who was, literally, captain of the football team and really chunky and really nice. I was relatively quiet and academic but he was very friendly and open with me. He went around with people who played rugby and swore and spat and that sort of thing and I thought they were horrible. But I thought he was great and very sexy and I could hardly keep my hands off him at times. He lived on Cumbrae and once when he was over for a football match he asked if he could stay with us. When it was time to go to bed I showed him his room and he said – can't you bring your bed down here and we can just have a laugh. This idea sounded fab but I was completely terrified and the situation was too difficult for me to handle. To him it was nothing but to me it was everything and I clammed up and just went up to my room. I don't think our friendship was ever the same again.

I went to Glasgow University and spent the first year in a hall of residence where everyone went around in packs. I joined the Operatic Society and was in a production of *The Gypsy Baron* and though I hated getting up on Sunday mornings I joined the University chapel choir. I didn't really make any close friends that year but there was one chap I met that I really liked and also fancied. He was the first person to say to me outright – are you gay? I denied it and because he was getting too close to the truth I distanced myself from him. There was an active Lesbian and Gay Soc. at the university but I didn't know anyone who was in it and I wasn't going to go along myself. But at the end of my first year I'd really got nowhere and I thought that if I wasn't going to make friends at university when was I going to make friends? I believed that if I told anyone I was gay everyone would gossip and the whole world would soon know. So I decided to tell my parents first.

That summer and the build-up to telling my parents was the unhappiest time of my life. I kept thinking that I needed to tell them but I didn't manage to do it before I started the next term. The first weekend of term I was back in Largs singing in the local church choir and I decided that this had to be the moment. I thought my parents might throw me out and so, just in case, I decided to gather together everything I might ever want from the house. I went round the rooms and put my clothes and memorabilia into a bag. On the Sunday morning I put the bag out in the porch. My parents were still in bed and I thought I'd catch them unawares while they were lying down. I went in and I was trembling – I really have to tell you I'm gay. They were quite shocked. My mum was upset but my father was okay and said that he'd met homosexuals when he was in the Merchant Navy. Also I'd never had sex at this stage and they're saying – well, how do you know you're gay? I'd known since I was fourteen and they couldn't really understand this. However they didn't throw me out of the house and when they weren't looking I sneaked my bag back from the porch into the bedroom.

My father had a theory that if I were to drink Guinness it would release my inhibitions and my 'normal' sexual urges would come to the surface. He tried hard to make me drink Guinness, but I was sceptical of the benefits, and anyway I hate the stuff. My parents found it very difficult to talk about my 'problem' and they thought

I should see a doctor. They came with me to see the doctor at the university and they went in without me and I went in without them. I don't know what he said to them but he asked me if I wanted him to give me the phone numbers of gay bars or places where you could meet people. I thought that was great but I declined because at the time it seemed like too much of a big step. He basically told me – and presumably my parents – not to worry about it. I was fortunate that I had a sussed doctor because if we'd gone to a doctor in Largs it could've been a different story.

It was such a relief having told my family, but at the end of that year I still didn't know any gay people. I also didn't know what I wanted to do with the rest of my life and very late that year I decided to do Honours French because I realised I would get to go abroad for a year. They had a place for me in Paris and I decided that I would 'come out' there. If I didn't like it I could come back and nobody would know anything about it. I had a fabulous time – picnics in the Bois de Boulogne, cheap restaurants, loads of shows and films, and I became involved in some theatre productions. It was such a great time that I more or less forgot about the fact that I was supposed to be coming out.

I did meet someone I fell in love with – a fellow student – and I just adored him. I couldn't work out whether he was gay or straight because I wasn't very good at that sort of thing. I had to tell him I was gay and take it from there. The night he was leaving I still hadn't told him and that evening I'd promised to go out for a meal with someone else. I was so nervous because of the task that lay ahead. In the restaurant I pretended to be feeling sick and said I would have to go home. I left her in town and then went over to his flat. It was nearly midnight and he was in bed. I got him up and told him I was gay. He said he wasn't. He knew I wanted to talk so he got dressed and we went for a walk over to the Île St. Louis. While I was getting (almost) everything off my chest over a cup of hot chocolate in a cafe, I couldn't help noticing a woman selling red roses to the two men at the next table. That was Paris for you. I decided at that point that I couldn't spend my life falling in love with straight men and therefore I had better start meeting other gay men. After that I met a few other gay people in Paris and this was a gradual build up to going back to Glasgow and sorting out my life.

I'd been corresponding while I was in Paris with Aileen Ritchie who'd been in my class. I told Aileen I was gay just after I came back and that was fine. She said I should get in touch with John Binnie who'd been a year behind me. I only knew him very vaguely but he was one of these people I presumed to be gay. We were in the same drama class now and we were friends right from the word go. We met up with another John who was also gay and the three of us started going out dancing. We hardly drank anything except water because we had so little money. I started to get to know other gay people and I don't know how I got a reasonably good degree because we spent so much time going out to *Bennets* or putting on shows.

I still hadn't had sex but I was determined to do so before my twenty second birthday. We were all going to St Andrews for the Scottish Student Drama Festival and there was somebody else in the cast whom I fancied and whom I knew to be gay, but I was too nervous to make a move. On the last night of the festival I went to a party in the Students Union where about three hundred people were doing Scottish Country dancing. I kept catching the eye of the guy that I fancied and eventually he came over and put his arms around me in the middle of the dance floor. I didn't really know what to do except the same back. A lot of people knew that we were both gay and they were really taken aback that we were so public. That didn't really bother us and we went back to the boarding house and changed the sleeping arrangements so that we could sleep together. I was very self-conscious and I was watching myself and watching him and copying what he did. I was so relieved to be able to say to myself that I'd done it but the earth didn't move. It was a bit awkward the next morning because everyone else had gone when we got up and we were sitting eating pork sausages and fried eggs knowing that everyone else was talking about us. But that was that phase of my life over.

After I left university I went down South, first to Sheffield and then to Birmingham. I worked in publicity and marketing at the *Crucible*. The day I went there a man introduced himself to me and we went on to become very close. We went out to films and clubs and I became his lodger and I felt like I was in a safe environment. When I went to Birmingham, on the first day I went into the office this woman whom I'd only just met said she had a friend who was looking for a lodger. She phoned him straightaway to tell him I needed somewhere to stay. She was on the phone to him and at the same time saying to me – do you smoke? No. Are you a vegetarian? No. Are you gay? I thought, do I say yes or no and I said 'yes'. I moved in that day. While in Birmingham I had a great relationship there with somebody who was very physically attractive. He picked me up one night when I was at a nightclub. I went home with him and we had a good night. We didn't make any plans to meet again. I bumped into him again at the club the following week. This time he was dressed as Tina Turner, in stilettos, black mini and fright wig. When I recognised him I said hello. He said hello and then immediately disappeared, coming back ten minutes later in his civvies. I went home with him again. It's maybe snobbish but I thought there wouldn't be much in common. Yet I liked spending the night with him and over the next two or three months if we were both out at the weekend we would spend the night together. Nothing was ever arranged but it was a great relationship and it really suited me at the time.

I'd kept in touch with John and Aileen while I was away and at Christmas 1988 I came back to work with them and Clyde Unity Theatre. I like working with Clyde Unity but to be honest I don't get a tremendous amount of satisfaction out of it. I design sets and do the publicity but I just always wish my own contribution could be better and I wish I knew how to improve the standard of my own work. The thing that keeps me at it is that I believe in everything the company stands for. It's good to do shows in Scottish accents that ordinary people can identify with and yet they offer an alternative view of society that says it's alright to be gay and it's alright to be fat and it's alright to love somebody who's not from your own country. I think a lot of writing in Scotland is entrenched in the myth of the Glasgow hard man and it's all seen from the point of view of the male heterosexual. It would be difficult for me to move to another company because there aren't really all that many companies that I admire.

During all this time that I have been having sex I have been aware that AIDS and HIV were around. I didn't throw myself into a mad fury of sexual activity – and that's partly my personality – because AIDS and HIV have always been at the back of my mind as a sexually active adult. That and a sort of insecurity about not knowing if you're in control of the situation when you're first meeting people makes me very reticent about sex. I like sex but I think that if I weren't in a steady relationship I would probably end up spending a lot of time not having sex. I know of many people who have died as a result of AIDS and there is no getting past the truth that the risk of sex, unless you are completely convinced that what you are doing is safe, is not worth taking.

In one sense it was a long time after I met Russell before I moved in with him. I first met him at a 'flexisex' disco in the QM Union and he was the first man ever to ask me to dance. I liked him a lot but he wore leather braces and I was a bit in awe of him. After that night I would say hello to him and we'd stop and talk on street corners and had I not gone off to Sheffield I might well have started to see him. I came up one Mayfest to see the *Mahabharata* and I met him at *Panamajax* and we spent the night together. When I was back living in Glasgow in 1989 I was sharing a flat with Aileen. She and I were both going through 'quiet periods' and we used to wonder if we would ever get boyfriends again. Once I told her then that I had decided to have an affair with Russell. Within days of saying that I met him in *Bennetts* and from then on I hardly spent another night in my own flat. I definitely wasn't looking for a serious relationship, but we've been together ever since and only on rare moments have I regretted it!

Now that I'm in a steady relationship my mum is very relaxed about it. It was obvious from the start that I was moving in with Russell and not just 'sharing a flat'. She was very quick to ask him down to Largs and now she always writes to invite him to join the rest of the family for Christmas dinner.

YVONNE

(b. 1967)

I was born in Glasgow in 1967, the youngest of a family of seven. When I was two we moved up North to Sutherland. It was quite rough in Pollok and I think my dad wanted a break from the city. He was a painter and decorator and he moved to an estate where he got a house as well. It was a tiny wee place and everybody seemed to be related and to know everybody else. We stood out; we were different and we were Catholics. We would have had to travel to Dornoch to say mass and so the priest used to come to our house. My mum's not really into the Bible but she is into the spirituality of the Church and Jesus Christ. It was important to her to have some connection to what she'd had in the city.

It was a complete change for the others but, at two, I didn't really notice it. There wasn't very much to do – go fishing, go walks, play cowboys or football. It was always outdoor stuff – using what was around us. I also used to play badminton on a Friday night in the hall. The shops were about fourteen miles away. I suppose I was quite sheltered being brought up there. When I was twelve, after leaving primary school, I was shipped off to boarding school in a convent in Perth. I would have had to have boarded at Golspie anyway but that would have been a bit nearer. I didn't want to be the only one that did something different but that's what my mum and dad wanted.

When I got there I quite enjoyed it and I was there for five years. I remember when I was leaving to go there my friend asked me if I was going to become a nun. I liked the nuns because they were nice people but I had no intention of becoming a nun. We had prayers or mass every morning; God was around in your whole daily life. It became such a part of your life you forgot about it. It was like having your breakfast – you did it and forgot about it. I got to know the other girls in my year quite well and we all just grew up with each other. They were all a lot richer than me and when I went to their houses at the weekends I would get paranoid about my own background. My accent changed completely and I became upper-class sounding.

I never did biology and so I never got taught anything about sex by anybody. There was talk of girls having relationships . . . or doing things with other girls, but I never did. I'd sort of known for a long time that I was gay but no one ever told me that this sort of thing happened to anyone apart from bad people, dirty girls. I knew that I wasn't a bad person or a dirty girl so I didn't think it was me. My mum was adding things up after I told her I was gay and she remembered me once asking her if she could send me back to God and make me a boy. From an early age I was sort of realising that I wanted to sleep with other women and I couldn't, but maybe if I was a man I could. I grew up and I just bided my time until I was free of school and family to do what I wanted.

I left school and around then it was all getting too much. I'd be about fifteen at the time when I told one of my older sisters. But at the same time I thought that I might be pregnant and so I was telling her that I might be pregnant and I might be a lesbian. She just looked at me like get one thing sorted out at a time and when I wasn't pregnant she just sort of forgot about the lesbian thing. Later I told my mum and she phoned up the Samaritans to work out what she should do with me. And through them, I wrote to this woman in Inverness and I thought that's all I had to do. It was like a big weight being lifted from my shoulders and I thought that everyone was going to be relieved that I'd found out what was making me depressed. They weren't. My mum was a bit shaky at first but she was really pleased that it wasn't anything else. My dad was quite shocked and I think he would have preferred it if I'd been on drugs. But that was just the first couple of days and they've come round now.

When I was nineteen, I packed up and came to Edinburgh with my wee bag. I knew people from school were living in Edinburgh but I wasn't really in touch with them. Eventually I got a bedsitter and from there I tried to find the scene. I ended up sitting in the dark and not even speaking to anybody and going out before anybody came in. I was doing my head in because I just wanted to meet people and I wasn't meeting anyone, straight or gay. I got a wee bit friendly with one of the guys living next to my bedsitter but that wasn't where I wanted to be. So I ended up phoning Lesbian Line but I got Gay Switchboard. I got one of the guys; for some reason it was much easier to talk to a guy. I was quite drunk at the time. He was really good and he made me realise that it was all going to take a bit of time. He told me about the women's nights at the *Guildford* and the women's discos at the *Duck* and through that conversation I felt a lot stronger. I met one of the women from Lesbian Line but it was all a bit strange. She was very like it wasn't a big deal but it was a big deal. I remember sitting downstairs at the *Duck*, gazing into my pint and I couldn't bear to look up. Then I plucked up courage one night and went to the *Guildford* on my own and it was through that that I got to know a core of people.

It all revolved round going to pubs and drinking and playing football and things like that. I moved from my bedsit into a flat with two other women. When I first moved there I remember getting a whole list – do you eat meat? do you smoke? do you have any male friends? I wasn't feminist, didn't really understand any of this but I went along with it, being a vegetarian and hating men. It definitely took off and it was so relaxed. I had friends and a place to live. I got a job with Gingerbread and I got to know people there who were quite lefty and not bothered about homosexuality. I was so excited about getting where I wanted to be.

There were just so many of us and we were all coming out at the same time. We'd all end up in one person's flat and stay there a while and then drift back to our own houses. It was all a bit mad, a bit hectic. You never knew who you'd find in the morning. Then I got involved with this older woman and that calmed me down. It took me out of the young, riotous, drinking, student group into this nice feminist type of life – eating at *Seeds* and that sort of thing. And, in a way, I dropped my younger friends. The scene is like that.

I moved to another flat and after I split up with the older woman I got involved with one of my flatmates. It was good on a lot of different levels and I came back to my own age group. I started to meet more men, gay men and straight men, and I like that contact. It was a relief to get out of the stereotype feminist/lesbian thing and come back to just being ordinary. A lot of my political life really left me and I went back to doing what I wanted. If I start to get put down as a woman, I definitely am a feminist but I've never read any feminist books. I rejected religion when I first came out but now I've taken on a wee bit of my mum's thing which teaches you what you are and the size of your spirituality.

I've always tried to be out in the places where I've been working but on the street you get clocked and I think that's the only time I've been aggressive and told the person to mind their own business. And I get taken for a boy a lot. I was working at an adult-training centre and I was showing a woman friend around when this guy came and said – Is this your girlfriend? I froze but then I realised that for the couple of months that I'd been there he'd thought I was a guy. I told him I wasn't a boy and so he asked if I was a man. We had a big discussion but he didn't connect that I was a woman. It's happened in the *Duck* too – I've been chatted up by gay men. Really bizarre.

There was one place where I was working where they got some cash and said I could make a film. I decided to try and make a film about lesbian painters. It became really difficult because it was all half-leads. I was going on things like women's paintings of other women, how they looked, what their job was, did they get married or did it matter if they did get married? Could they still have been gay if they were married? I did speak to one woman painter – straight, I think – and she said it was irrelevant if someone was gay or not. But I just wanted for that so much not to be the case. I was so determined that it must have something to do with the way they painted or who they painted or something to do with their life as a lesbian. I got fascinated for a while by the painter, Gluck. She was an amazing-looking woman and she posed for male photographs. Then again, I wanted something Scottish and Joan Eardley was the only Scottish woman painter I could find. In the end I ran out of time. It's really a lifelong project and the whole thing just fell to pieces.

I am a student on a drama and stage management course now. In our year there's six of us who are out and so it's no big deal. It's not hostile and people are fascinated, if anything, by the whole thing. People have done their own writing and there's one woman who's written a lesbian play or a play with lesbian bits in it. It seems to be a good thing for me in this particular year. I could go anywhere when I've finished the course. But I'd like to stay in Scotland. I couldn't see myself going down South. We'll just have to see how the jobs go.

ROY SCOTT

(b. 1968)

I was born in Dundee on Boxing Day in 1968. I stayed in Forfar until I was sixteen with my parents and my older brother. Forfar's a small market town with some textile factories. There's only about ten thousand people and so everyone knows everyone else. No one in my family had particularly strong religious or political beliefs but we were sent to Sunday School when we were young. Then it was up to us what we wanted to be in terms of religion.

My first sexual experience was in Primary Seven – just the usual stuff, trying to find out what the other's got. But I never really thought about it until I was in second year at secondary school. The big gay scene in Forfar seemed to be in the local dramatic societies and opera societies and that was how I started to meet other men and boys my own age. My first formal sexual experience was when I was about thirteen or fourteen. There was one guy who was in the same year, but not the same class, as me and we were rivals in terms of the dramatic society. Although we had this love/hate relationship, we saw each other on a regular basis and I suppose we sort of loved each other. I also had one or two small experiences in the toilet in the old Cross building.

There was nothing mentioned at school about the possibility that you might not be the 'normal' student. All you learned about being gay was derogatory but I never had any problem with it. I got a lot of name calling at school but I didn't care. I was friendly with one guy who was camp and anybody he associated with was labelled as homosexual. I never worried about it. When I was fourteen we had this French student over and I had a crush on him and I wrote him imaginary wee letters. I had no intention of sending them but my mum found them but I fobbed it off by telling her that she didn't have very good French and that one word was 'girlfriend' and not 'boyfriend', like she thought. There was one time when I was about fourteen or fifteen when I was forced to do something sexually that I didn't particularly want to do and I was bleeding quite badly. I thought that I could be dying but there was no way I could turn to the family and say 'Mum. . . . '

I actually had a coming-out party just after I left school. One of the girls from the dramatic circle had a birthday party in the Royal Hotel and I went to it. I knew I was leaving and there were loads of girls and a guy that I was close to and I wanted to tell them. I had started seeing somebody from Edinburgh and we danced together and we got quite a few raised eyebrows. But when we danced together for the slow dance, there were quite a few of the girls in tears. They were upset with me about the fact that I'd never told them before and we were supposed to be friends. There was actually this girl from Arbroath that I was going out with for about a year and a half and it was all – 'How could you use me like this?' But there were guys in my year who started speaking to me in the street whereas before they would just have walked past me. I seemed to get more respect for speaking up for myself.

About that time I was doing stuff for Radio Tay. They gave up an hour's air time each week to young people so that they could air different views and we decided to broach the subject of homosexuality – a first for Radio Tay. We did research and we had to go to a disco and try and find people who were willing to speak. It was me and this girl. She was on one side of the room and I was on the other and we were both enjoying ourselves. Eventually we twigged on to each other and we were going – I didn't know you were/I didn't know you were. We did two programmes. One was about a lesbian and her mother going to the gay disco together; the second part of that was about a guy being chucked out of his house. The other programme had a piece on gay music crossing into the mainstream and a discussion which touched on AIDS.

After one of these programmes I was on the bus home to Forfar and I was thinking – I want to tell Mum. My mum and dad had been away on holiday at the time of the party in the Royal Hotel. The programme made me think I had nothing to lose. I saw that my mum was up, which was unusual, because normally by that time she would be in bed. She said – I heard your programme tonight – and then she said – Are you gay? I went uh-huh – just like that. No hesitation. She went – I never expected you to say 'yes'. I thought I'd really have to wangle it out of you.' She was obviously quite upset at the time but after that she was fine.

My mum decided she wasn't going to tell my dad and she didn't want me to tell him. There is about an eighteen-year difference between them and she reckoned he wouldn't understand. It was two or three years later when I told him and his reaction was – that's fine; I knew all along; when I was in the Army it didn't bother me but I don't particularly want to talk about it. My brother said he knew too. My mum's from a big family, eleven brothers and sisters, and she's very close to one of her sisters. That auntie said my mum had spoken to her about it and that she was fine but she was concerned about AIDS.

I have a gay uncle and maybe that helped. When I was about thirteen he came up from England where he stays and we were going round visiting places in a car he had hired. I was starting to realise about myself and I was suspicious of him. Like I would never go to the toilet at the same time as him but then when he came back I would make some excuse and go on my own. He asked me what the problem was but it was difficult to talk about then. I was just starting to find out about myself and I just didn't want to face up to the possibility of him being gay. We started talking about it later but I only saw him occasionally because he lived down South. There was no great coming-out session. We both just realised.

After I did my Highers and left school, I went to Edinburgh for a few months. That was when I really ventured out on the scene. We would go out for a drink and then on to *Fire Island* and I would dance till it closed. At that time I thought discos were just for dancing. We'd go to someone's house for coffee and back to my flat to get ready for work. God knows when I got to sleep. That's all I did – go out and enjoy myself.

I wasn't sure what I wanted to do careerwise but I took the plunge and took an acting job in Orkney for six or seven months. None of the other actors were gay but they were quite happy about it. I met a guy who had lived there since he was five and we went out for six months. It was still iffey for two guys to dance together but we did it all the time. The summer school I was working on was for children around the fourteen/fifteen age group and they came from Thurso, Caithness, Shetland and places like that. They were there for two or three weeks and they stayed at the school hostel. I was wearing pink triangles at the time and they started wearing them too. I said – I don't think you should be wearing pink triangles quite yet. But they said that they were open-minded and that they completely understood. Everybody was fine about it except for some guys from the TA. But from what I heard about some of them, they hardly had anything to talk about.

When I was in Edinburgh I really didn't think about things, but I had done in Orkney and I had been totally open and I'd had such a good response. When I came down to Dundee again, it wasn't a problem. That was when I met a guy who I lived with for three years. I was still only seventeen and I think he realised that if he tried to pin me down I would just rebel. So it was a vague relationship but we understood each other. All his friends and his family accepted us as a couple. We started to live together in Dundee and after six months we moved to Glasgow. I was selling computers there. I worked for two companies while I was there. The first one was small, just two or three people, and so I didn't have to hide my problems or anything I had been doing. I'd only been with the second company two weeks when we split up after a three-year relationship.

I met someone else from Dundee and after I was offered a job in Dundee I moved again. I moved in with him and his family. When we visited my family in Forfar we would get to share a room together and my brother would be chucked downstairs. But my brother and his girlfriend were never allowed to share a room. I found that quite amusing. The whole family accepts me now. It's quite funny with my gran. She's almost eighty and when I was through in Forfar a wee while ago she apparently said – Is that your new boyfriend? But everyone thought they had misheard her and just ignored it. She was embarrassed because she thought I might take offence.

I still live in Dundee and I tend to socialize around work. I am the Training Officer for a ten-pin bowling company and I suppose it is a bit of a man's world. I am always surprised with the late hours that there aren't more gay men working there but it's not been a problem for me.

The gay scene in Dundee is very small and I always feel I'm being scrutinised. It's difficult too if you've had one or two relationships; people can be bitter and there is only one pub. There are sometimes problems with disco hours and licensing and I wish people would stand up for themselves. I can't understand why some people are so secretive. There is an SHRG group here but they don't do much. I would feel more inclined to join ACTUP because they actually get off their arses and do something.

I've never felt the need to move down South. My current boyfriend is Indian and comes from London but I wouldn't live down there. One of our plans is to move to Australia when he has finished studying here. He would be able to get in as a doctor and Australian immigration laws would allow me to be admitted as his partner. That'll be the first time I've lived outside Scotland.

I've never really had hassle about being gay. I get all sorts of comments but it doesn't worry me. I've never had any problems about being worried about gay-bashing. I always remember a phrase – it's better to be hated for what one is than loved for what one is not.

SHAHBAZ CHAUHDRY

(b. 1969)

I was born in Glasgow on February 27th 1969. I'm a Pisces. My father had just become a bus-driver when I was born. He had been a lawyer of some kind in Pakistan and then when he came here he and his brother opened a shop. He wasn't the happiest of men at the best of times and he certainly wasn't happy about becoming a bus-driver. When I was born my mother became asthmatic and so I wasn't viewed with the loving eyes of my parents. I have three brothers and one sister and I was the fourth one. We were Shia Muslims and being brought up in a fundamentalist Islamic culture didn't help me very much in this Western culture.

A lot of my memories are of being chastised or beaten. But when

I was about six or seven I went to Pakistan for six months and that was a very happy time. We went to stay with my mother's family in Lahore and I remember feeling very loved, very wanted. I saw much more of the gentle side of my mother and even my father never really gave me a hard time. I remember thinking that we were just outside Glasgow when we were in Pakistan at first. It's really open there and I'll never forget these huge toads. I remember seeing this huge lump and I thought it was a pile of mud and then it leapt up and I got such a fright. We went to a mosque too with a beautiful minaret and we went to the top of the minaret and there was a prayer call and it was a wonderful feeling. I looked down and there were flowers and I'll never forget the smell and the fragrance. It was a wonderful time.

I remember being happy at school and not being happy at home. Schooldays were the best days of my life because I remember being happy and playing games and not being picked on. I think people felt sorry for me because there was a wee sad air about me. I was called a poof because I had this fixation with Linda Carter who was Wonderwoman. She was my superhero and I would twirl around in the playground and pretend I was Wonderwoman and chase everyone. That was one of the first camp things I remember getting into. Although I didn't get on with my big brothers at home, it was always easier at school and they would defend me. I made friends with the older lads too and if anyone began to pick on me they would go and sort them out, which I quite liked. I managed to strike a balance for myself and spent 50% of my life in fantasy and 50% in agony. I was the upset child at home and the court jester for everybody outside.

I was about eleven or twelve when I reported my family to the school authorities. I just couldn't hold back any longer, couldn't go on lying about what a wonderful family I had and I burst into tears. I was taken to the Guidance Room and I showed the Guidance teacher the bruises on my arms. Social Work intervened and things got better for a while but I was hated because I had embarrassed my family. Things did get a bit easier at home but my academic qualities suffered terribly and to this day I find it hard to concentrate on anything academic.

I still enjoyed school and I was the cabaret artist of the playground. I was about thirteen or fourteen when the New Romantic period started and my biggest influence was Marilyn. I was becoming a young man and I still had no homosexual experience at all and I wanted to grow my hair like Marilyn. I didn't fancy him but I was inspired by him. My father wouldn't allow us to watch things like 'Top of the Pops' and so I would sneak off to somebody's house to watch it when Marilyn was going to be on. I used to go to school and it would be a riot when I started singing these Marilyn records. I never had a hard time at school. I was this wee Asian with glasses and I wanted to be Marilyn. People at school would call me a poof but I still didn't really understand that, though I was behaving like Marilyn and was obviously very camp. I'm sure now that my parents could see that side of myself. I started to fancy two boys in my class. If people called me a poof I just began to ignore them. I knew I wasn't doing anything bad and I began to close off all the negativity. I began to discover around this time that there were people who would accept me for what I was and people who wouldn't. I am what I am and if some people can't accept that they can go straight to hell.

I spent a lot of time when I was fourteen buying pop magazines for the Marilyn pictures and also Marilyn records. I used to do the messages for my mother and I would steal some of the money so that I could buy these Marilyn things. I would dodge school and I would go for wee adventures to Hillhead library. I'd walk into town and there I was in Buchanan Street. I went wild. I'd been so closed off. I'd once thought that Pakistan was just around the corner but Buchanan Street was another world. I made pals in record shops and they would order me my records. There was another boy in my class and we became pally and we would exchange Boy George pictures and Marilyn pictures. We were always getting into trouble and I became quite bitchy and would talk back to my teachers. I had fantasies about one of my teachers and I was masturbating a lot. I'd taken enough shit and I became a bad boy.

I wanted to be loved a lot and I made other kids' mums my surrogate mothers. My sixteenth birthday passed uncelebrated and I was really angry with my family. So I packed all my bags and I left home on March 1st 1985. I went to a hairdresser's near me and one of the guys lent me three or four pounds and told me to go to Maryhill Social Security Office. I didn't know anything and I went from place to place and eventually ended up in a Homeless Unit. I still stayed on at school.

It was around this time that I had my first cross-dressing experience. There was this old blue dress left around and I got into tights and I was singing Marilyn records as usual. After two weeks I was thrown out of the hotel for being a wee poof, basically. It was a big struggle but I had got my allowance book and my independence.

I'd thought all my troubles were over but they were really just beginning. I was doing Marilyn Monroe impressions as well as being Marilyn and I got beaten up in one hotel. I went back to the hairdresser's I was pally with and I got them to bleach my hair pure blonde. I went to school with it all lacquered and blue eye-liner and Monroe lips. I was so busy exploring my sexuality that I wasn't getting anywhere academically and I decided to leave school. My mother was in hospital at this time and when I went to see her she got a real shock.

After this I started to go out on the scene. I went to *Vintner's* first and then one Tuesday night I went to *Bennett's*. This man spoke to me and I was getting really horny. I was getting really randy and tingling all over and I didn't really understand it was sex creeping up on me. Eventually he took me to his home. It was beautiful, like a little art gallery with fancy furniture and big leopard skin rugs. I was a fast learner and I was giving him oral sex by the morning. He was a nice man and he took me home. But when I got back to my room I felt really dirty, as if I'd done something wrong, and I had a bath. But it wasn't long after that that I started to attract men. I shaved my legs and I was walking down the street, cross-dressed and in high heels. I was picking up men like it was nobody's business. But it certainly wasn't all fun. A man in my bed and breakfast took a shine to me; a shine that I didn't really like. Eventually he raped me and beat me up. It was a horrible experience and I was totally traumatized. I became a bit unbalanced and slept in closes for a while. I also began buying dresses and jewellery with a stolen credit card. I ended up being given two years probation. I went back to the Homeless Unit and began to pick up the pieces. Eventually I was offered my own place and though it was pretty heavy at first I've been there for six or seven years now.

I really believe in self-expression. I am a spur-of-the-moment queen by the way I dress. I'm quite a performer and I had dreams to become a pop star. I made my first record in 1987 and it was called *Outrageous*. Then I made my first video which was quite an achievement because I realised I was following in the footsteps of Marilyn and my other heroes. Basically I was a big gay act and people said they just don't sell that easily.

I've experienced a lot of racism. I've been called a dirty Paki poof and I've learned to ignore that. I think that I'm just like anybody else. But people do point out my nationality and my colour and, I must admit, a lot of that is on the gay scene. Edinburgh's much more cosmopolitan but Glasgow is a really screwed up, backward sort of place. They all live by what other people think and an individual like me just stands out like a sore thumb. Some of the people on the Glasgow gay scene are great and I love them but I feel I've outgrown them.

Time's been a great healer as far as me and my family are concerned. I know that my mother's a lovely person and though I still have some resentment about my childhood I don't blame her anymore for what happened. My sister left home recently and we get on better now because she understands more about where I am coming from. I get on alright with the brother who's just a bit older than me. It's amiable and we're on slightly better than speaking terms. And my little brother and I have always been close.

In the last few years I've got into a very close friendship with a lady called Linda. She's good to me. She has a fifteen year-old daughter, Zeinab, who has cerebral palsy and I've learned a lot from her. She's severe in her disadvantage but she doesn't suffer from prejudice or bias or bigotry. She only knows love. I've learned to be more accepting through my contact with them. I don't want to become contorted and bitter. I want to help people accept each other. We're all here for such a short time that it's important that we just live together. It is important but I feel that people will not accept others until they accept themselves for whatever they are.

APPENDIX 1

Contact list

There are now many meeting places and organisations for lesbians and gay men in Scotland. There are groups for lesbian mothers, trade unionists, Christians, hillwalkers, people who are HIV Positive, football supporters, young people and many more. The phonelines listed here can provide you with information about these and about bars and clubs. They can also offer counselling and befriending in some cases. If there is no phoneline near where you live, it is worthwhile phoning one of the others for information about your local area.

Phonelines

ABERDEEN   Lesbian, Gay and Bisexual Switchboard
                  0224 586869.   Wednesdays 7–10 pm

DUMFRIES	Gay Group 0387 69161. Thursdays 7–10 pm
EDINBURGH	Gay Switchboard 031 556 4049. Every evening 7.30–10 pm
EDINBURGH	Lesbian Line 031 557 0751. Mondays, Thursdays 7.30–10 pm
FIFE	Friend (Kirkcaldy) 0592 266688. Fridays 7.30–10 pm
FORTH	Friend (Stirling) 0786 471285. Mondays 7.30–10 pm
STRATHCLYDE	Gay and Lesbian Switchboard 041 221 8372. Every evening 7–10 pm
STRATHCLYDE	Lesbian Line 041 353 3117. Wednesdays 7–10 pm

Youth groups

Stonewall youth group meets weekly in Edinburgh 031 556 4040. Tuesdays 7.30–9 pm.

Strathclyde Lesbian and Gay Youth Movement meets twice weekly. Write PO Box 69, Glasgow G4 0TY or phone Strathclyde Switchboard.

West and Wilde Bookshop Wide range of books, magazines, etc. Also mail order. 25A, Dundas Street, Edinburgh EH3. 031 556 0079. Open daily.

Gay Scotland Monthly magazine produced by and for lesbians and gay men in Scotland. 58A Broughton Street, Edinburgh EH1 3SA. 031 557 2625.

Outright Scottish lesbian, gay and bisexual rights campaigning group. 58A Broughton Street, Edinburgh EH1 3SA.

Scottish AIDS Monitor (SAM) PO Box 48, Edinburgh EH1 5SE.

APPENDIX 2

Notes for a Homosexual map of Scotland

T he following places were all mentioned in the original interviews which took place for this book. They referred to places where lesbians and gay men had been born, where they lived, where they had visited, where they had made love, where they had had sex. This list may prove a useful starting point for any cartographer intending to produce a homosexual map of Scotland. It certainly goes some way to confirming the slogan that lesbians and gay men are everywhere.

A

Abbeyhill
Aberdeen
Airdrie
Alloa
Anniesland
Arbroath
Ardrossan
Argyll
Auchtertool
Ayr

B

Ballingry
Bathgate
Beauly
Berwick
Blairgowrie
Blantyre
Brechin
Bridgeton
Bruntsfield
Buckie

C

Caithness
Cambuslang
Cardenden
Carluke
Carntyne
Coatbridge
Corpach
Cowdenbeath
Crieff
Cumbrae
Cumnock

D

Dalkeith
Dornoch

Drumchapel
Drumnadrochit
Dumbarton
Dumfries
Dunblane
Dunfermline
Dundee
Dysart

E

Easterhouse
East Kilbride
East Lothian
Edinburgh

F

Falkirk
Falkland
Fife
Forfar
Fort Augustus
Fort William

G

Galashiels
Garngad
Glasgow
Govanhill
Greenock

H

Harris
Hawick
Helensburgh
Hyndland

I

Inverness
Irvine